BILLY GRAHAM

Hear My Heart

WHAT I WOULD SAY TO YOU

HOWARD BOOKS
A Division of Simon & Schuster, Inc.
New York   Nashville   London   Toronto   Sydney   New Delhi

Howard Books
A Division of Simon & Schuster, Inc.
1230 Avenue of the Americas
New York, NY 10020

First Howard Books hardcover edition April 2014

HOWARD and colophon are trademarks of Simon & Schuster, Inc.

For information about special discounts for bulk purchases, please contact Simon & Schuster Special Sales at 1-866-506-1949 or business@simonandschuster.com.

The Simon & Schuster Speakers Bureau can bring authors to your live event. For more information or to book an event, contact the Simon & Schuster Speakers Bureau at 1-866-248-3049 or visit our website at www.simonspeakers.com.

Designed by Davina Mock-Maniscalco

Manufactured in the United States of America

10 9 8 7 6 5 4 3 2 1

Library of Congress Cataloging-in-Publication Data

Graham, Billy
Hear my heart : what I would say to you / Billy Graham.
    pages cm
1. Christian life—Baptist authors. I. Title.
    BV4510.3.G73 2013
    248.4—dc23
                                        2013004152
ISBN 978-1-4767-3430-9
ISBN 978-1-4767-3431-6 (ebook)

Contents

PART THREE: GUARD YOURSELF

PART FOUR: MY CHALLENGE TO GOD'S PEOPLE

I had a Hindu student say to me in Madras,
"I would become a Christian if I could see one."
And when he said that to me, he was looking at me.
That was one of the greatest sermons ever preached to me.

—BILLY GRAHAM

Introduction

AMERICA'S PASTOR GOES HOME

By Marshall Shelley

Billy Graham was perhaps the most significant religious figure of the twentieth century, and the organizations and the movement he helped spawn continue to shape the twenty-first.

During his lifetime, Graham preached in person to more than two hundred million people and to millions more via television, satellite, and film. Nearly three million responded to the invitation at the end of his sermons to "accept Jesus into your heart." He proclaimed the gospel to more people than any other preacher in history. In the process, Graham became "America's pastor," participating in presidential inaugurations and speaking during national crises such as the memorial services following the Oklahoma City bombing and the 9/11 attacks.

"He became the friend and confidant of popes and presidents, queens and dictators," said Columbia University historian Randall Balmer, and yet even in his later years he possessed "the boyish charm and unprepossessing demeanor to communicate with the masses."

Billy Graham was born in 1918 in Charlotte, North Carolina. He briefly attended Bob Jones College, graduating from Florida Bible Institute near Tampa and Wheaton College in Illinois. He was ordained a minister in the Southern Baptist Church in 1939; he pastored a small church in suburban Chicago and preached on a weekly radio program. In 1946 he became the first full-time staff member of Youth for Christ and launched his evangelistic campaigns. For four years (1948–1952) he also served as president of Northwestern Schools in Minneapolis. His 1949 evangelistic tent meetings in Los Angeles brought him to national attention, and his 1957 New York meetings, which filled Madison Square Garden for four months, established him as a major presence on the American religious scene.

Graham appeared regularly on the lists of "most admired" people. Between 1950 and 1990 he won a spot on the Gallup Organization's "Most Admired" list more often than any other American. *Ladies Home Journal* once ranked him second only to God in the category "achievements in religion." He received both the Presidential Medal of Freedom (1983) and the Congressional Gold Medal (1996).

Sherwood Wirt, who for seventeen years edited the Graham organization's *Decision* magazine, cited one Scottish minister who made this observation about Graham: "My first impression of the man at close quarters was not of his good looks but of his goodness; not of his extraordinary range of commitments, but of his own 'committedness' to his Lord and Master. To be with him even for a short time is to get a sense of a single-minded man; it shames one and shakes one as no amount of ability and cleverness can do."

Graham was a model of integrity. Despite scandals and missteps that toppled other leaders and ministers, including Graham's friend Richard Nixon and a succession of televangelists, in six decades of ministry no one ever leveled a serious accusation of misconduct against him.

That's not to say he wasn't seriously criticized. Some liberals and intellectuals called his message "simplistic." Some fundamentalists considered him "compromised" for cooperating with mainline groups and the National Council of Churches. His moderate antisegregationist stance during the civil rights era drew fire from both sides: white segregationists were furious when he invited the "agitator" Martin Luther King, Jr., to pray at the 1957 New York City crusade; civil rights activists accused him of cowardice for not joining them on protest marches and getting arrested for the cause.

In 1982, when he visited the Soviet Union to preach the gospel at the invitation of the government, he touched off a firestorm of criticism. Despite having met with the Siberian Seven—Pentecostal dissidents who were seeking political asylum—Graham was quoted as saying he "had not personally seen any evidence of religious persecution." Some called him a traitor. But he insisted he would go anywhere to preach as long as there were no restrictions on his freedom to proclaim the gospel. He returned claiming he saw the hand of God working in the Soviet Union. He was fiercely attacked for being naïve and "a tool of the Soviet propaganda machine."

By 1990, however, after the fall of the Soviet Union, his prescience was vindicated when President George H. W. Bush said to the National Religious Broadcasters, "Eight years ago, one of the Lord's great ambassadors, Rev. Billy Graham, went to Eastern Europe and the Soviet Union and, upon returning, spoke of a movement there toward more religious freedom. And perhaps he saw it before many of us because it takes a man of God to sense the early movement of the hand of God."

Perhaps Graham's lasting legacy was his ability to present the gospel in the idiom of the culture. He did this brilliantly, making innovative use of emerging technologies—radio, television, magazines, books, a newspaper column, motion pictures, satellite broadcasts, the Internet—to spread his message.

In the 1990s he re-engineered the formula for his "crusades" (later called "missions" out of deference to Muslims and others offended by the connotation of "crusade"). His standard "youth night" was revolutionized into a "Concert for the Next Generation," with Christian rock, rap, and hip-hop artists headlining the event, followed by Billy Graham preaching. This format drew record numbers of young people who cheered the bands and then, amazingly, listened carefully to the octogenarian evangelist.

In addition he helped launch numerous influential organizations, including Youth for Christ, the Billy Graham Evangelistic Association, and *Christianity Today.* The ripple effect of his shaping influence extends to such schools as Wheaton College in Illinois, Gordon-Conwell Divinity School in Massachusetts, Northwestern College in Minnesota, and Fuller Seminary in California. His encouragement and support helped develop the Evangelical Council for Financial Accountability, Greater Europe Mission, Trans World Radio, World Vision, World Relief, and the National Association of Evangelicals.

He brought the global Christian community together through international conventions: a 1966 Congress on World Evangelism in Berlin; the 1974 International Congress on World Evangelization in Lausanne, Switzerland; and three huge conferences in Amsterdam for itinerant evangelists in 1983, 1986, and 2000, which drew nearly twenty-four thousand working evangelists from two hundred countries.

In many ways, Billy Graham both formed and embodied the evangelical movement. Theologian J. I. Packer attributes the evangelical "convergence" to Graham: "Up to 1940 it was every institution for itself. There wasn't anything unitive about the situation. There were little outposts of resistance trying to keep their end up in the face of the liberal juggernaut. Increasingly, from the 1950s onward, evangelicals came together behind Billy Graham and the things he stood for and was committed to. It continues that way to the present."

For many, however, William Franklin Graham won't be remembered for these accomplishments. He'll always be "Billy," as he preferred to be called. He titled his autobiography *Just as I Am,* a reflection of his humble spirit, taken from the hymn sung most often when he invited people to come forward and receive God's love. And for millions, his humility before the Almighty encouraged them to approach God with that same spirit.

May this book, which in so many ways represents his heart to us all, encourage you to do the same.

—Marshall Shelley

Vice President, *Christianity Today*

Part One
WHEN GOD CALLS

GLOBAL CHAMPION
OF THE PURE GOSPEL

By J. I. Packer

Theologian J. I. Packer is the Board of Governors' Professor of Theology at Regent College. The best-known of his many books is Knowing God *(1973). He was general editor of the English Standard Version of the Bible and has long served as one of* Christianity Today's *top advisers. He has known Graham since 1952.*

I n March 1952, while still a layman, I was fortunate enough to be invited to a gathering of 750 evangelical leaders, not-quite-leaders, and not-yet-leaders at Church House in central London to hear a thirty-five-year-old American evangelist, Billy Graham, speak and answer questions about his crusade ministry in the U.S. His address—based on Habakkuk's prayer that God would revive his work—developed the theme that in the remarkably fruitful large-scale missions that he had been leading, God had been doing precisely that.

Graham was relaxed, humble, God-centered, with a big, clear, warm voice, frequently funny, and totally free of the arrogance, dogmatism, and implicit self-promotion that, rightly or wrongly, we Brits had come to expect that American evangelical leaders would exude. He was engaging in his style and displayed as he spoke the evangelist's peculiar gift of making everyone feel that he was talking personally to him. He monologued for ninety minutes and answered questions for another hour. Though somewhat prejudiced at that stage of my life against all forms of institutionalized mass evangelism, I ended up admiring the speaker and very glad that I had been squeezed into the meeting. In retrospect, it stands in my memory as something of a landmark.

The agenda item, to which this meeting was a preliminary, was whether to invite Graham to lead a crusade in London. Two days after the meeting where he had wowed, the invitation was issued—the first step on the road to Harringay, the most momentous religious event by far in twentieth-century Britain. Hundreds, perhaps thousands, of lasting conversions spinning off into dozens of vocations to evangelical pastoral ministry led to high morale and significant spiritual advance through the next generation, despite the juggernaut inroads of national secularism in British public and community life. That Billy Graham, under God, left his mark on England for good is not open to doubt.

In spiritual things, when you are being attacked on both sides, you are probably positioned right.

It has been said that in spiritual things, when you are being attacked on both sides, you are probably positioned right. Graham came to England in the 1950s. During the time when his most significant work there was done (Harringay, and evangelistic addresses in England's key universities), he was under constant fire in America for not being a combative, noncooperative fundamentalist. In England, however, he found himself consistently opposed by Anglican and Free Church leaders (chiefly Anglican, as a matter of fact) who railed at him for being precisely that, and therefore a thoroughly undesirable influence on the British scene.

Those were the days in which so-called "liberal" and "critical" orthodoxy—a contradiction in terms, really—ruled the roost in Britain's theological teaching centers, and the image of evangelicalism in leaders' minds was of a crude, standoffish, individualistic, unscholarly, and indeed antischolarly distortion of the historic faith, always underappreciating God's kingdom and God's church. The history of evangelical defensiveness against liberal landslides on both sides of the Atlantic during the early years of the twentieth century sufficiently explains where this caricature came from. And as for "liberal/critical orthodoxy," it is now clear that, so far from being a benchmark and standard of alert faith—as it thought itself to be—it was a comprehensive shaking-off of the Christian commitment to the objective authority of biblical teaching. As such, it was a first step down the slippery slope into naturalistic relativism and subjective speculation. Once one plants even one foot on that slope, slipping and sliding become the order of the day, checked only by comfort-zone willpower.

Contributions to the debate by John Stott, myself, and others had some success in making this clear, thus vindicating Graham's own stand for the full inspiration and authority of the Bible; and today it is widely if not universally recognized that his reverent revelational biblicism is, was, and always will be the authentic Christian approach to the task of determining God's truth. And liberalism, though stubbornly entrenched in many places, languishes, and indeed has almost totally lapsed as a Christian nurturing force. At the same time, the Christ of the Scriptures, as evangelicals acknowledge him, has in the past half-century gone forth conquering and to conquer, with increasing global impact in Africa, Asia, South America, the U.S., and (though less spectacularly) in Britain and Canada.

As for historic fundamentalist divisiveness, the critics found they had nothing to fear from their American visitor. Avoiding denominational issues altogether, Graham always practiced evangelism cooperatively, enlisting all—including Roman Catholics—who would join him in proclaiming personal salvation according to the Scriptures.

Graham's British breakthrough was epoch-making. It was the first step of a truly global ministry, which he sustained for more than a generation, bringing authentic biblical Christ-centered Christianity—that is, Christianity in which Christ's cross, resurrection, present reign and future return, salvation through him, obedience to him, and hope placed in him are central. Graham's remarkable empathy, whereby he identified in need and caring terms with every community he visited, added to the sense of Christlike authority in his substantially unchanging proclamation. It also had a unifying effect, both theologically and attitudinally; shared embrace of "the gospel Billy Graham preaches" became a bond of fellowship between Christians of different stripes and backgrounds all around the world. Graham became a bridge figure, linking together all sorts and conditions of Christians through himself in bonds of common evangelistic and nurturing endeavor that hopefully will remain now that he is gone.

A comparable impact was made by Graham's initiatives in bringing together evangelists from around the world for mutual encouragement, prayer, and focusing the ongoing missional task (evangelism, church-planting, Christian nurture, and relief of need) in this constantly changing world, and in the face of the sociopolitical reconceiving of mission that the World Council of Churches sponsors. The global gatherings at Berlin, Lausanne, Manila, and Amsterdam have been landmarks, both in bringing together larger global representations of evangelicalism than ever before, and also in providing guidelines for evangelistic strategy (statements, books, research, resources, and most notably the Lausanne Covenant) marking out the path forward with clarity and an unprecedentedly broad consensus. Here, too, Graham's vision and enterprise moved global evangelicalism forward, leaving it less parochial and more ecumenical than it was when he came to it.

Hats off, now, to thank God for his gift to us of this great man.

2

WHAT IT MEANS
TO BE "BORN AGAIN"

The nineteenth and twentieth centuries were times of great scientific advance. Those multiplied decades brought us such marvels as jet power, nuclear power, television, and modern missiles, as well as many hundreds of gadgets that add to the comfort of mankind."

Science gives us all these things, but it does not tell us what to do with them. At this point we must have moral and spiritual resources in order to use properly the things science has created.

Give an immature boy an air rifle and he may shoot out the windows. Give the morally immature human race hydrogen bombs and missiles and they may blow the entire world to bits. Science has led us to the possibility of a Golden Age, but science has also brought us to the possibility of the destruction of the human race. Man stands at the crossroads; he must make a choice.

The word *Christian* is of Latin derivation. Literally it means "partisan of Christ" or "a member of Christ's party." The one thing you can say about partisans, whatever their politics, is that they are never neutral. They never play it safe; they never sit on the fence; they are never spectators in the struggles of their time. They throw in their lot. They commit themselves. They hear and follow their leader, come what may. So the very word *Christian* implies a commitment of life, a decision, a choice.

Christ told us that we do not have the inner resources to face the problems, frustrations, and crises of life. We need new resources that he alone can provide. He said, "You must be born again" (John 3:7 NKJV). Jesus taught clearly that unless we experience a new birth or conversion, we cannot enter the kingdom of God.

The sense of futility in life seems common to many and is understood by almost everyone. Even the young people of today seem to share this feeling of futility. Several years ago, the Johns Hopkins alumni magazine asked 291 graduating seniors to submit essays appraising and defending their own generation. The apathetic result was a single reply that came from a twenty-six-year-old Navy veteran, a history major. Among other things he said, "We are resigned to a position of grayness and indecision. If my generation seems inert, it is not because we do not care; it is because we feel helpless. We are not so much lost as rootless." The feeling of futility produces an apathy toward the moral issues of our day and unconcern over fraud and dishonesty in high places. This attitude on the part of the public is more frightening than the transgressions against decency and integrity themselves.

Man desperately needs the moral and spiritual certainties that faith in God can bring him. When modern man feels himself to be a cosmic orphan—adrift on a planet precariously balanced in space, without a personal God as his Father, without a future life to which he may aspire—then it is easy for his life to splinter when it encounters the hard problems of our troubled times.

When Jesus Christ was on earth, he was concerned about bringing wholeness into the lives of those he met. He taught that man can be born again. He made this statement to a scholar by the name of Nicodemus. If Jesus had said, "Except you, Nicodemus, be born again, you cannot see the kingdom of God," we would have written it as a statement to one particular person with no general application. But Jesus used a generic term: "Except *a man* be born again, he cannot see the kingdom of God" (John 3:3, emphasis added).

Immediately Nicodemus raised a question: "How can a man be born when he is old?" (John 3:4). He was not so much interested in the new birth itself as in the way it worked. He wanted to view the matter objectively. He asked, "How can a man . . . ?" rather than, "How can I . . . ?" He had a tendency to argue himself out of the new birth rather than to believe himself into it.

Dr. Carl Jung, the great psychologist, once said, "All the old, primitive sins are not dead but are crouching in the dark corners of our modern hearts." Jesus indicated that something is wrong with the human heart when he said, "Those things which proceed out of the mouth come forth from the heart; and they defile the man" (Matthew 15:18).

Psychologists realize that something is wrong with the human race. Some call it a constitutional weakness; the Bible calls it sin. The Bible describes sin as the free act of an intelligent, moral, responsible being asserting himself against the will of his Maker. It has affected every part of our lives, even our minds.

Clearly, if imperfect man is to reconcile with a perfect God, a change is needed. Jesus addressed this change when he said, in effect, "Nicodemus, you are scholarly, you are religious, you have position and power; but unless you are born again, you cannot see the kingdom of God."

All through the Scriptures runs the truth that a change is needed. Ezekiel said, "A new heart also will I give you, and a new spirit will I put within you" (36:26). In Romans, Paul speaks of it as being "alive from the dead" (6:13). In 2 Corinthians he calls it being "a new creature: old things are passed away; . . . all things are become new" (5:17). To the Ephesians he said that they had been "quickened," or made alive from the dead (2:1). In Titus it is called "the washing of regeneration, and renewing of the Holy Ghost" (3:5). Peter calls it being made "partakers of the divine nature" (2 Peter 1:4). In the Church of England's catechism it is called "a death unto sin, and a new birth unto righteousness." The new birth brings about a change in disposition, in affection, in design. New aims, new principles, new dimensions of life can be yours if you put your faith and confidence in Jesus Christ.

The new birth is a mystery accomplished by the Spirit of God. When the children of Israel had been bitten by snakes in the wilderness as a judgment, thousands of them were suffering and dying. God told Moses that he should make a serpent of brass and hold it up to the people and that those who would look at the serpent would be healed. Moses held up the brass serpent. Many looked and were healed. But many refused to look. It was an insult to their intelligence; there was no healing quality in the brass. But God had said it. They did not have to rub ointment on their sores. They did not have to minister to others who had been bitten. They did not have to fight the serpent or make an offering to the serpent. They did not have to look to Moses. They just had to look to the brass serpent in faith and beyond the serpent to God (Numbers 21:8–9).

So Jesus said, "I am going to be lifted up. Look unto Me, and be saved" (see Isaiah 45:22). Our generation could be saved by a look of faith to Jesus Christ.

Science and medicine can help. Psychiatry can help. But our ultimate salvation is at the cross of Christ, where he died for our sins and where all the possibilities of a new dimension of life exist. If we will look, we will live.

3

HOW TO KNOW YOU ARE SAVED

In the First Epistle of John, fifth chapter, thirteenth verse, we read: "These things have I written unto you that believe on the name of the Son of God; that ye may know that ye have eternal life, and that ye may believe on the name of the Son of God." That is the reason this epistle is written to the people. "These things I write unto you," said John, "that ye may know that ye have eternal life."

Now I ask you, do you know whether you have eternal life? What do I mean by eternal life? I mean life here and now, a full-orbed life, life's complete fulfillment, as well as heaven to come when you die. Do you know that you have that? The Bible says you can know it. You can be sure of it. John says, "These things I write unto you that believe on the name of the Son of God; that ye may know that ye have eternal life." A Christian who has received Christ can say with assurance, "I know that I have eternal life. I'm sure. I have received Christ. There are certain evidences in my life that indicate that I've passed from death unto life. Whether I was conscious of the moment or unconscious of it, I've passed from death unto life and I know that I'm ready to meet God. I know in whom I have believed."

> *I've passed from death unto life and I know that I'm ready to meet God. I know in whom I have believed.*

All through the epistles, the apostles say, "I know." You can know; you can be sure. Paul said, "I am persuaded . . . I know these things." How can you know? How can you be sure?

PERSONAL EXAMINATION

Well, I want to give you an examination. I want to ask you some very pointed questions about your own life. The Bible says that God's law is a mirror. And when I look into the law, the Ten Commandments, or the Sermon on the Mount, the Bible says that I see my true self. I see how I appear in the sight of God. The Bible says that God does not judge the outward appearance. I'm not asking about your financial status, about the latest fashion in which you are dressed, about your social position, about the color of your skin, or about your cultural background. I'm asking, *How do you stand in relationship to God?* Are you sure that you have eternal life?

The rich young ruler came to Jesus and said, "What must I do to have eternal life?" What did he mean? He meant that he wanted the best out of life here, that he wanted full-orbed living. Now, he had religion. He had culture. He had education. He had everything that would normally make a person happy. But there was an empty spot in his life. He knew that there was something else in life that he didn't have, and so he came to Jesus. But, he asked something else. He wanted to know about life after death. He wanted to know whether he was going to live with God forever. He wanted to know about this life that Jesus was talking about when he said, "I have come to bring life, more abundant life."

SOURCE OF LIFE

The Bible teaches that God is from everlasting to everlasting. God is life. Jesus said, "I am the way, the truth, and the life" (John 14:6). *Life:* Life with a capital *L*. That is, *spiritual life*. Now, there is physical life. Physically you are alive. Spiritually, the Bible says, all of us are dead and separated from God. Take the illustration of a lovely plant. I cut off a stem and it lies on the floor. The stem looks just as healthy as it ever did from the outside, but the sap can no longer come into it, and eventually it will die because it is separated from life. That is exactly what sin does. Sin has cut the lifeline between you and God, and God speaks of us as spiritually dead. Separated from God. Cut off from God's fellowship. Separated from life.

Now, God is life. The moment you come to Jesus Christ and receive him, the Bible says you are grafted back into the vine. Jesus said, "I am the vine, ye are the branches" (John 15:5). You are grafted in as a branch. The Bible says you become a partaker of eternal life—spiritual life—and immediately something happens. The Bible says the sap, the spiritual life of God, begins to flow through you, and evidences appear that you have spiritual life. You don't go on as a dead plant, as a dead branch. The leaves begin to sprout. Certain things begin to take place in your life. This life of God is yours, and the Bible says you will live as long as God lives. When the stars have fallen, when the moon has fallen out of its orbit, we'll still be living because God is from everlasting to everlasting, and those of us who have spiritual life in Christ Jesus shall live forever. Oh, it's wonderful to be a Christian! And that's the thing that the world cannot understand. That's the thing that a person who has never received Christ cannot understand. He doesn't understand that flowing through you now is the life of God, giving you power, strength, and the dynamic to live the Christian life.

MAKE SURE!

Do you have the life of God flowing through you? Have you received spiritual life through Christ? You should check to see whether you have life. The Bible speaks in Hebrews 10:22 about the full assurance of faith. The blind man said, "One thing I know, that, whereas I was blind, now I see" (John 9:25). Make sure! Can you say, "I was blind to spiritual things, but now I see. I was once dead to spiritual things, but now I have life. I was once in spiritual darkness, but now I'm walking in the light"? Can you say that? If not, I beg of you to come to Christ and make sure.

Has there been a moment when you received Jesus Christ as your Lord and Savior? Paul said to the Philippian jailer, "Believe on the Lord Jesus Christ, and thou shalt be saved" (Acts 16:31). "No, Paul," you say, "that's an oversimplification. You're too simple, Paul. You should have given him something complicated to do. Paul, you should have told him all that's involved." But Paul didn't. Paul said, "Believe." Why? Because believing—if you understand the word properly—is the entrance, the beginning of new life in Christ.

THE MEANING OF FAITH

Now, what does it mean to believe? The word *believe* involves your intellect. We must know Christ and accept his claims. Christ claimed that he was the Son of God, that his death on the cross was the only way to heaven, that he was God incarnate. You must accept Christ in all that he claims, or put him down as one of the biggest liars, hypocrites, and charlatans in history. I had to decide in my own heart and in my own mind that Jesus Christ was what he claimed to be. I made my decision years ago. I stood at the crossroads and intellectually made this choice. I said, "O God, by faith with my mind I accept the fact that Jesus Christ is what he claimed to be and that when he died on the cross, it was not the ordinary death of an ordinary man but it was God in Christ reconciling the world unto himself. It was Christ shedding his blood for our sins."

ACCEPTING CHRIST WITH YOUR ENTIRE SELF

First is the intellect. Second is emotion. Emotion is involved in everything we do. You cannot separate emotion from the mind and the will. Love is emotion. Hate is emotion. When I come to Jesus Christ, I love Christ because he gave himself for me on the cross, and I hate sin. Hate and love are emotions. I have very little time for a person who can sit in front of a television set and weep and laugh over a sitcom or go to a ballgame and shout, "Kill the umpire!" and yet condemns emotionalism in religion.

The third factor is the will. Thousands of people are in churches today who accept Christ with the intellect. The Bible says that the devils believe and tremble. We haven't done much trembling. Some of you have had emotional experiences in religion as a child, as a young person. But you still do not have spiritual life until a third thing takes place. Here is the important thing: you must by an act of your will receive Christ.

When I stood before the minister to get married, he said, "Wilt thou take this woman to be thy wedded wife?" I said, "I will"—publicly, before everybody in that church, as scared as I was, by an act of my will. I didn't answer him and say, "I believe in Ruth and I love her." That was not it. I had to say, "I will." Leading up to that moment there had been weeks and months of courtship. I used every tactic that I'd ever heard about or read about to win her. However, we were not committed to each other until we said in front of the minister, "I will." Then the transaction was recognized in the courts of heaven and earth.

When you come to Jesus Christ it is also an act of your will. That is involved in that little word *faith*. I believe. I receive Christ by faith. It is an act of your will when you commit your life to him. Have you done that?

FORSAKING SIN

After receiving Christ, did you forsake sin, the known sin in your life? Lying, cheating, immorality, pride—all of these things? Now that doesn't mean you had total and complete victory over them every moment. But it does mean that you began to turn from sin. Sam Jones, the great evangelist, said that his church used to say, "Quit your meanness." That's what it means to follow and serve Christ. "Let the wicked forsake his way, and the unrighteous man his thoughts: and let him return unto the Lord, and he will have mercy upon him" (Isaiah 55:7).

Suppose I have a pig. I give him a bath in suds. Then I take his hooves and put nail polish on them. Then I take a little Chanel No. 5 and put that on his back. I put a beautiful ribbon around him, bring him into the living room, and seat him on my sofa. He sits there and he smells and looks sweet. A beautiful house pet! Everybody says, "Isn't it wonderful? What a lovely pig you have. Isn't he a nice, sweet pig? I've never seen such a lovely pig." I open the door and let the pig out. Where does he go? He goes back to the mudhole, because his nature has never been changed. He's still a pig.

You can take a man, dress him all up on Sunday morning. He puts his little halo on his head, sprouts his wings, and he goes in and sits down in the church. He smiles and beams all over. Twelve o'clock comes. He walks out, shakes hands with the minister, smiles, and says, "It was wonderful this morning, Reverend." Then, about midafternoon, the halo comes off, the wings are moved aside, the horns begin to grow, and he picks up his pitchfork again for another week. He goes back and practices the same old sins. His nature has never been changed. That is the reason Jesus said, "Ye must be born again." You must have a new heart, a new soul, a new direction in your life.

OBEYING CHRIST

Another way to check yourself is to determine whether you obey Christ. Do you have a real desire to obey? He said, "He that hath my commandments, and keepeth them, he it is that loveth me" (John 14:21); "And hereby we do know that we know him, if we keep his commandments" (1 John 2:3); "If a man love me, he will keep my words" (John 14:23); "He that loveth me not keepeth not my sayings" (John 14:24).

Do you obey Christ? Do you obey him by reading his Word? Do you obey him by spending time daily in prayer? Do you obey him by being faithful and loyal to the church? Do you obey him by giving your tithes and offerings for the support of the work of the Lord?

I've had hundreds of people say, "Billy, I have no spiritual blessing. I have no spiritual power." Always I start asking, "Do you read the Word?" Nine times out of ten they answer no. "Do you spend time in prayer?" "Oh, yes, I pray every day." "Well, do you tithe your income?" "Well, no. I haven't done that very well." "Do you mean that you expect God to bless you when you're robbing God?" Every denomination teaches tithing. Why? Because it is based on the Old and New Testament rules of giving. We are to give to the Lord, and we rob him when we don't.

THE FRUIT OF THE SPIRIT

Another way to check yourself is to determine whether you have the fruit of the Spirit. The Bible says the fruit of the Spirit is love, joy, peace, longsuffering, gentleness, goodness, faith, meekness, temperance (Galatians 5:22–23). Jesus said, "Ye shall know them by their fruits. Do men gather grapes of thorns, or figs of thistles? . . . A good tree cannot bring forth evil fruit, neither can a corrupt tree bring forth good fruit" (Matthew 7:16, 18).

I want to ask whether you possess the fruit of the Spirit. The moment you receive Jesus Christ as Savior, the Holy Spirit comes into your heart. Your body becomes the temple of the Holy Spirit. The moment you receive Christ, the third person of the Trinity—the Holy

Spirit—comes to live in you and produces fruit. Spiritual life begins to flow. The leaves begin to come out. The fruit begins to bear in its season. You have love. "By this shall all men know that ye are my disciples, if ye have love one to another" (John 13:35). "We know that we have passed from death to life, because we love the brethren" (1 John 3:14). The whole Scripture is filled with one glorious triumphant word that is to characterize every child of God—*love*.

The Blessing of Joy

Another fruit of the Spirit is joy. When I see a fellow going around with a long face and his shoulders all stooped over with the burdens of the world, I know that man knows nothing of the filling of the Spirit of God. The Bible says believers are filled with joy. Listen, a Christian is to have a smile on his face, a spring in his step, and joy in his soul. That is the Christian life. Paul and Silas were in jail and had been beaten on the back until they were bleeding, and at midnight they were singing! Regardless of circumstance, if Christ is in your heart, you can smile, you can sing. There is joy and there is peace through the Holy Spirit.

Peace of Soul

Peace is also a blessed fruit. There is an inner serenity. The greatest picture of peace I've ever seen was on the North Carolina coast. A storm was raging. The wind was blowing, the sea was lashing, and the thunder was roaring. Under the crevice of a rock was a little bird. It had its head under its wing, asleep. That's peace—the peace that God can give. Let the storm rage. I have peace because I know the Prince of Peace.

Are you bearing the fruit of the Spirit? If you are not fruit-bearing, it may be that you have never been grafted into the nature of God and become a partaker of God's nature. You had better check to be sure. Are you sure this day? The Scriptures say, "These things have I written unto you that believe on the name of the Son of God; that ye may know that ye have eternal life" (1 John 5:13). Do you know it? Are you sure? Are you certain? You can be sure by presenting yourself to Christ and receiving him as your Lord and Savior.

4

God's Love

L ike Wesley, I find that I must preach the law and judgment before
I can preach grace and love.

The Ten Commandments are the moral laws of God for the conduct of people. Some think they have been revoked. That is not true.
Christ taught the law. All those commandments are still in effect
today. God has not changed; people have changed.

Every person who ever lived, with the exception of Jesus Christ, has
broken the Ten Commandments. Sin is a transgression of the law. The
Bible says "all have sinned, and come short of the glory of God" (Romans 3:23). The Ten Commandments are a mirror to show us how far
short we fall in meeting God's standards. And the mirror of our shortcomings drives us to the cross, where Christ paid the debt for sin. Forgiveness is found at the cross and no other place, according to the Bible.

God says, "Thou shalt have no other gods before me" (Exodus 20:3). You may not have any idols set up in your back yard, but there are idols in your life. Anything that comes before God is your idol. You spend more time reading the newspaper than you do reading the Bible. You spend more time in front of the television set than you spend in church. Idols have crowded God out of your life. You just don't have time for him anymore. Another commandment says, "Thou shalt not take the name of the Lord thy God in vain; for the Lord will not hold him guiltless that taketh his name in vain" (Exodus 20:7). You may not curse God, but you take his name in vain when you profess to be a Christian and don't live like one. You take his name in vain when you defile your bodies, when you make vows and don't keep them, when you pray and don't believe God.

You may not curse God, but you take his name in vain when you profess to be a Christian and don't live like one.

The Bible says, "Honour thy father and thy mother" (Exodus 20:12). Young people today think this is old-fashioned. God doesn't think it is old-fashioned. He commands that such respect be given. The Scriptures say, "Thou shalt not kill" (Exodus 20:13). You may not have broken this commandment with a gun or a knife, but you have broken it. If you have ever had hate in your heart, you are guilty. You can murder your own souls by denying or neglecting God. You can murder others by setting a bad example.

Another commandment says, "Thou shalt not commit adultery" (Exodus 20:14). You may not have committed the act, but the Bible says if you have ever looked on a person with lust in your heart, you are just as guilty. A woman commits this sin when she deliberately dresses in such a way as to entice a man. Preachers have been silent for too long on the subject. America can be destroyed quicker by moral deterioration than by foreign threats.

The Bible says, "Thou shalt not steal" (Exodus 20:15). It isn't necessary to use a gun in order to break this commandment. We rob God in tithes and offerings, in our daily devotions, and in not observing the Lord's Day as we should. God also says, "Thou shalt not bear false witness against thy neighbour" (Exodus 20:16). The disgrace of the Christian church today is that we don't have love for one another. May God have mercy on those who publish the secular magazines that will murder a man's reputation in order to print a sensational story. May God have mercy on the leaders of some Christian periodicals who spend all of their time trying to expose other Christians.

All have broken these commandments. All have sinned, and death is the penalty, but Christ paid the debt when he died on the cross. If you will come to the cross, confess and renounce your sins, receive the Lord Jesus by faith, and surrender your will to him, he will forgive and forget. You will become a new person in Christ. Then you begin to grow as a Christian when you read your Bible, spend time in prayer, witness, and become active in your church.

We have the law to show us we need God's love. But Christ's death on the cross atoned for our lawbreaking. When we preach atonement, it is atonement planned by love, provided by love, given by love, finished by love, necessitated by love. When we preach the resurrection of Christ, we are preaching the miracle of love. When we preach the return of Christ, we are preaching the fulfillment of love. The answer to our problem of lawbreaking is ultimately God's love for us.

5

GROWING AS A CHRISTIAN

Who is a Christian? A person is not a Christian because his parents were godly people. Christian parents are wonderful, but they can't make the decision for a child. He must do it himself. A person is not a Christian just because he is sincere. My mother thought she was giving me cough medicine once, but she had unknowingly poured out some poison. She was sincere, but she was sincerely wrong.

A person isn't a Christian just because he follows his conscience. His conscience may be dead. You aren't a Christian because of your feelings. Feelings change.

Then who is a Christian? I'll tell you. *A Christian is a person in whom Christ dwells.* The Scripture says, "Christ in you, the hope of glory" (Colossians 1:27).

A Christian is a person who believes that his sins have been forgiven through the shed blood of Jesus Christ. The devil will try to make you doubt this. How can you know your sins have been forgiven? Because God said so, and God can't lie.

A period of adjustment follows the decision to live for Christ. Your life has been changed. Christian growth must begin unless you are to remain a spiritual baby. Some people never grow spiritually, and many of our churches are filled with babies. These people are among the most miserable on earth, because they don't feel at home with Christ and they don't feel at home with the world. They want both, and it doesn't work.

How does a Christian grow? I am going to list five ways. There are others, but these are five of the most important.

GROWING THROUGH PRAYER

First, a Christian grows when he prays. When you were a baby, you had to learn to walk. You learn to pray the same way. God doesn't expect your words to be perfect. When I heard my son Franklin say "Da-da" for the first time, the words were more beautiful than any ever used by Churchill. I would have been a little worried, however, if he had still been saying "Da-da" when he was twelve years old.

It's a shame that our churches are practically empty for Wednesday night prayer meetings. Some people think they have to be emotionally moved to pray before the prayer is really meaningful. The person who

waits to pray until he feels like it will never pray—the devil will see to
that. The Bible says you are to "pray with-
out ceasing" (1 Thessalonians 5:17). This
means that you can be in a spirit of prayer
while driving your car, walking down the
street, working in the office, or wherever
you may be.

> *The person who waits to pray until he feels like it will never pray.*

Every Christian should have a quiet time alone with God every
day. Your spiritual life will never be much without it.

Prayers should be filled with praise to God, with thanksgiving for
all the wonderful things he has done. Self-examination should be in
your prayers as you confess shortcomings. God is interested in hearing
your personal requests, no matter how small. You should seek guidance in prayer. An important thing to remember is that you should
pray that God's will be done and not your will. People make mistakes.
God doesn't.

GROWING THROUGH BIBLE READING

Second, a Christian grows when he reads the Bible. This should happen every day, without fail. The Word of God cleanses the heart. Many
people don't read the Bible because they don't understand it all. I want
to tell these people that they will never understand all the Bible. I
passed a big milestone in my own Christian life one day when I knelt
before God and confessed there were many things in the Bible I didn't

understand, but that I was going to accept it all as the inspired Word of God, by faith. From that moment, the Word became a living fire in my soul.

Turn off the television set and read the Bible. Begin in the New Testament if you're a new Christian; it's easier to understand. Don't read to see how many chapters you can cover. It's better to read two or three verses and meditate upon them.

Make sure you have a Bible with large print. One of the devil's biggest tricks is to have Bibles with small print so people won't read them. Though I use the King James Version by long habit, I would recommend that most people use a good modern-speech translation.

GROWING THROUGH SELF-DISCIPLINE

Third, a Christian grows when he leads a disciplined life. Your body, mind, and tongue should be disciplined. Practice self-control. The Holy Spirit will give you the strength to become Christian soldiers.

Many temptations will come to do battle with such discipline, but in Christ you can resist. The Bible says, "There hath no temptation taken you but such as is common to man: but God is faithful, who will not suffer you to be tempted above that ye are able; but will with the temptation also make a way to escape, that ye may be able to bear it" (1 Corinthians 10:13).

The tempter will flee when you answer with a verse of Scripture. It's impossible to argue or rationalize with the devil. Jesus, the Son of

God, answered temptation by saying, "It is written . . . "A little boy expressed it very well one day when he said, "Every time temptation knocks, I just send Jesus to the door."

GROWING THROUGH CHURCH ATTENDANCE

Fourth, a Christian grows by being faithful in his church. Going to church is not optional; it's necessary. God says we are not to forsake the assembling of ourselves together.

Lots of people today don't go to church in the summer because it is too hot. In the winter they don't go because it is too cold. I'm afraid I don't know the ideal church temperature.

Many figure that the preacher is doing a fine job if he doesn't go five minutes beyond twelve o'clock. But if that happens, they are ready to get another one. It may surprise some of you to know that you don't go to church just to hear a preacher. You go to worship God.

Get into a good church where the Bible is preached and Christ is exalted. Get to work for God. Join a group Bible study in your church. Invest time, energy, and study into church and good fellowship with Christians, and you'll be surprised at how your dedication to God deepens.

GROWING THROUGH SERVICE

Fifth, a Christian grows through service. Be a soul winner. There's a difference between a witness and a soul winner. Anyone can walk up to another on the street and bark, "Brother, are you saved?" It takes more than that. A soul winner is filled with the Spirit of God. He visits the sick. He gives to the poor. He loves his enemies. He is kind to his neighbors. He wins people by passing on God's love, not by trying to add another star to his spiritual accomplishments. We have a lot of witnesses today but very few soul winners.

Do these five things and you will find yourself living the Christian life as God would have you live it, and you will discover that you have become obedient to Christ's command, "Thou shalt love the Lord thy God with all thy heart, and with all thy soul, and with all thy strength, and with all thy mind; and thy neighbour as thyself" (Luke 10:27).

Part Two

THE POWER
OF THE GOSPEL

6

A LIFE OF DEVOTION

By John N. Akers

John Akers was academic dean of Montreat College until 1977 when he began his work with Graham. Over the years, he worked with Graham on research, administration, and special projects—especially coordinating trips to China, North Korea, and Eastern Europe. He was editorial coordinator for many of Graham's published works, including his "My Answer" newspaper column and his autobiography, Just As I Am.

N o doubt future historians will find more than enough material from Billy Graham's life and work to keep them occupied for generations. One of the main questions they will want to answer is: what was the secret of his success? And no doubt their answers will range from the sublime to the ridiculous, depending on the depth of their research and their personal biases and even the academic fads of their day.

But one of Graham's secrets will probably elude most of them: his deeply felt commitment to a consistent, thoughtful devotional life. Without it, Graham never would have become the person he was, nor would he have had the worldwide impact he did. It kept him humble, reinforced his integrity, expanded his vision, and enabled him to keep his focus. Most of all, as he often said, it kept him close to the One he sought to serve.

There was nothing unusual about the elements of Billy's devotional life: the Bible, prayer, and reflection. In his view, each was essential, and each was bound up with the others. Like millions of other Christians, he had learned early the value of setting aside a definite time each day (preferably in the early morning) to be alone with God, a practice he sought to maintain even in the midst of overwhelming pressures, disruptions, and frequent travel.

I suspect he first learned, or at least sensed, the importance of private devotional time from his mother, Morrow Graham. She was a literate and spiritually minded woman who, after meeting some devout Plymouth Brethren neighbors who encouraged her to take the Bible more seriously, made a point to carve out time slots in her daily farm duties to pray and read her Bible.

After his conversion, Billy accepted for himself the importance of daily quiet time, a practice reinforced during his Bible college years. He often said that his time at Florida Bible College was the most important period of his life in terms of his spiritual growth. There he learned what it meant to study the Bible systematically and thoughtfully, and the experience shaped his life in profound ways.

Throughout his evangelistic ministry he encouraged new converts to establish a daily time with God (alongside becoming active in a church where they could grow spiritually). Those who came forward in the crusades received a simple Bible study and other materials to facilitate this.

Graham's relationships with his teachers and fellow students at Florida Bible College and Wheaton College also helped shape his mind and soul—a pattern that continued the rest of his life. One of his most significant personal qualities was his willingness (even eagerness) to interact with men and women whose education or experience might help him expand his horizons—from his wife, Ruth, and her father, Dr. L. Nelson Bell, to theologians and churchmen as diverse as Harold Ockenga, Carl F. H. Henry, Karl Barth, and the archbishop of Canterbury. He enjoyed few things more than the opportunity—all too rare, given his visibility—to slip unnoticed into a church service and hear someone else preach. He filtered their views through his understanding of the Scriptures and of God's will for his ministry as an evangelist, but his willingness to learn from others (even his critics) is often overlooked.

Billy maintained the practice of setting aside a daily time for Bible study and prayer to the end of his life. It would be wrong, however, to conclude that he restricted this to once a day. Prayer was a constant part of his life (even while preaching or talking with someone), and he frequently opened his Bible or spent time reflecting on what he felt God was teaching him whenever he had a free minute. He often asked visitors if they could end their time together with prayer, even as his health declined. As his sight deteriorated he found it increasingly hard to read anything more than a brief passage from the Bible, and that only with very large, computer-generated print.

Why was a disciplined devotional life so much a part of his life? It wasn't mere habit, nor was it because that was what any sincere Christian was supposed to do (although these had their place). Nor was it simply a desire for intimacy with God—although that was important to him. Beyond these were two other reasons for his devotional habits.

First, Billy Graham took seriously the apostle Paul's question: "Who is equal to such a task?" (2 Corinthians 2:16 NIV). Faced with the enormity of the responsibilities (and opportunities) he felt God had set before him, he knew that in himself he was not equal to the task, and he needed God's help. Yes, God had called him and gifted him as an evangelist, but that was not enough. The words of Jesus echoed through his soul and sent him to his knees: "I am the vine; you are the branches. If a man remains in me and I in him, he will bear much fruit; apart from me you can do nothing" (John 15:5 NIV1984). Even a casual reading of his autobiography, *Just as I Am*, repeatedly demonstrates this sense of dependence.

The second reason for his devotional habits was equally compelling: Billy Graham had a deep concern—even a fear—that he might do something (even inadvertently) that would bring disgrace to the name of Christ. As a young man he had seen this happen to evangelists and other Christian leaders who allowed sin—pride, sexual misconduct, strife, lovelessness, hypocrisy, cynicism, lying—to creep into their lives. He was determined it would not happen to him. In private he frequently quoted God's warning to Isaiah: "I will not give my glory to another" (Isaiah 42:8 NIV1984).

One response was the brief list of commitments he and his early associates drew up even before their ministry was widely known: purity in personal conduct, integrity in finances, honesty in statistical reporting, and cooperation with local churches. But the other answer, he knew, was to stay immersed in the Scriptures and only move forward prayerfully and in humble reliance on God. Billy Graham's legacy will be debated for decades, perhaps centuries. But one of his most enduring legacies should be the one that was largely hidden from public view: a life of humble devotion to his Savior and Lord, Jesus Christ.

7

THE BOOK THAT GIVES LIFE

Among us preachers there is a tendency to read the Bible for ammunition, and it is indeed the great sourcebook for our preaching. But it is much more. It is strength, and it is sustenance.

Through my years of experience I have learned that it is far better to miss breakfast than to forgo a session with God's Word. It's not that Bible reading is some kind of religious fetish bringing good fortune, but that I lack decisiveness and purpose and guidance when I neglect what is more important than the food that is necessary for my body.

For many years I have made it a practice to read five psalms and one chapter of Proverbs every day. The psalms show me how to relate my life to God. They teach me the art of praise. They show me how to worship—how to dwell "in the secret place of the most High" (Psalm 91:1).

The book of Proverbs shows us how to relate our own lives to our fellow men. The first verse of Scripture I ever memorized was taught to me by my mother from the book of Proverbs: "In all thy ways acknowledge him, and he shall direct thy paths" (3:6). These twelve words formed the foundation for the faith that later transformed my life.

I find that unhurried meditation on the Word of God is of great value. When in the morning I read a chapter and meditate upon it, the Holy Spirit brings new shades of meaning that are thrilling and illuminating. Sometimes his Word makes such an impact on me that I have to put the Bible down and get up and walk around for a few moments to catch my breath.

If the Bible does not inspire us in the privacy of our rooms, then we can be assured that our messages will not move those who listen to us preach. If it does not reach *our* hearts, it will never reach *their* hearts. If it does not stir us, it will never stir our hearers.

Our family's day at home always began with Bible reading and prayer. I know it is old-fashioned, but so are breathing, eating, and sleeping. The people who helped us around the house joined the family, and together we read a portion of God's Word, meditated upon it, made a comment, and then had prayer.

On my desk are many things—a telephone, a dictating machine, a pen, and a Bible, among other things. They are on my desk because they work. The Bible is the one indispensable item. If ever I get to the place where the Bible becomes to me a book without meaning, without power, and without the ability to reprove and rebuke my own heart, then my ministry will be over, for the Bible has been far more than my necessary food.

8

HOW CHRIST
FREES AND UNITES US

It is important for Christians to regularly examine the person and work of Jesus Christ as found in the Scriptures in order to determine just how Christ frees us and unites us. Let's explore the three questions that arise from this theme:

WHO IS JESUS CHRIST?

This question echoes and re-echoes throughout the New Testament and is still the central question facing people today. The Christian faith is centered in the person of Jesus Christ.

Who is this Jesus? We must guard against remaking Jesus to fit our

own ideas. Too often men have attempted to remold Jesus and the
Scriptures to make them conform to the concepts and presuppositions
of contemporary secular thought. This

*We must guard against
remaking Jesus
to fit our own ideas.*

can never be done, however, without
undermining the Christian faith.
There is only one Jesus—the historical
Jesus of the Scriptures. In the Scrip-
tures we learn the good news of the gospel, that God—the infinite,
personal Creator of the universe—has invaded this planet in the person of Jesus Christ. Supernaturally born in a minor province of the
Roman Empire, this Jesus lived a sinless life and through his actions
demonstrated God's love for all men. He was put to death on a
Roman cross, but because of his bodily resurrection, believing people need no longer fear the powers of sin and death and hell.

WHAT DOES IT MEAN TO SAY
THAT JESUS CHRIST FREES?

We are both freed *from* something and *to* something. The Bible declares
that man has rebelled against his Creator and has become enslaved by
sin. The effects of this rebellion can be seen everywhere, from the bro-
kenness of human lives to the corruption of human society. Ultimately,
all human problems—both individual and social—spring from man's
rejection of God's plan for humanity and man's attempt to find fulfillment apart from God.

The good news of the gospel is that God, in his love, has acted in Christ to free men from their bondage to sin and death and hell. The death of Christ on the cross was the most significant event in history. Through his sacrificial death, Jesus Christ made it possible for all people to be freed from a life ruled by sin and freed to a life ruled by Christ. To all who will repent of sin and turn to Christ in trusting faith and obedience, the risen Christ in his grace promises forgiveness and life, both now and eternally. It is one of the glorious mysteries of the gospel that an individual can only find freedom as he or she becomes a bondservant of Jesus Christ.

The freedom that Christ brings must never be confused with secular aspirations for political or social freedom, valid as they might be. The freedom Jesus brings is spiritual, and the Christian knows that this is the ultimate need of all people. Therefore, while fighting for social justice at every opportunity, the Christian will also seek to proclaim the release from spiritual bondage offered by Christ. Jesus rejected the radical schemes of the Zealots of his day, not because they were too revolutionary but because they were not revolutionary enough. He knew people could have political freedom and still be enslaved by sin and guilt. Only as they recover the purpose for which God created them can true freedom come.

WHAT DOES IT MEAN TO SAY
THAT JESUS CHRIST UNITES?

The Bible says that one of the catastrophic effects of humanity's prideful rebellion against God is alienation. This has two dimensions. Man is alienated from his Creator, and he is alienated from his fellow man. In Jesus Christ, however, God has brought about the possibility of reconciliation of both man with God and man with man. Through faith in Christ people are reconciled to God; they become a part of the church, which consists of all people who share a common loyalty to the Jesus Christ of Scripture.

One of the fruits of the Holy Spirit in the life of the Christian is love. The Christian no longer is to see others from a human point of view, whether they be Christians or non-Christians. Instead, he or she is called to see others as God sees them and to seek to minister to their needs in the name of Christ. He or she is called to be united together in purpose and love with all who are serving Christ. He or she is called also to declare by word and act the good news of the gospel to those who are outside the people of God, beseeching them to become reconciled to God.

It is my prayer that all who bear the name of Christ will search the Scriptures afresh and discover there in a deeper way Jesus Christ, the freedom giver and uniter.

9

REKINDLING OUR PASSION
FOR THE LOST

Where are our tears for the lost? Where is our concern for those who are confused, frustrated, lost, sinful, and destined for hell? At times it seems people will allow any detail to undermine attempts to reach those who are lost and dying. An example was our New York campaign of 1957, which was challenged by some extremists on two points.

First, it was challenged as to its sponsorship, which included the Protestant Church Council in New York City. This council included members with a decidedly modernist view of Scripture. I would like to make myself quite clear. It was always my intent to go anywhere, sponsored by anybody, to preach the gospel of Christ if there were no strings attached to my message. I was sponsored by civic clubs, universities, ministerial associations, and councils of churches all over the world. Not one person in New York even suggested or hinted as to what my message should be. It was precisely the same message that I had preached all over the world. The centrality of my message was and always will be *Christ and him crucified.*

Second, we were challenged many times on what happens to the converts when the crusade is over. Apparently the brethren who made these statements had no faith in the Holy Spirit. The work of regeneration is the work of the Holy Spirit. The work of follow-up is the work of the Holy Spirit. The same Holy Spirit that convicted those people of sin and regenerated them is able to follow them. No group of ministers in any large city anywhere in the world ever agreed on what constitutes a sound church. We did all we could in follow-up, but ultimately all converts are in the hands of the Holy Spirit. *He is more than able to nurture them toward maturity.* We have overwhelming evidence of how miraculously the Holy Spirit has led thousands who have come forward in the meetings to surrender their hearts to Christ.

This picking at detail and failure to see the big picture of the need to save lost souls tells me that many have lost their passion for evangelizing the lost. This loss shows itself in several ways:

The lost sensibility to the majesty of God. We handle holy things too glibly and professionally. We need to sense the majesty and holiness of God, as did Isaiah, Moses, and Daniel. If we could get a glimpse of God today, we

> *We handle holy things too glibly and professionally.*

would fall on our faces as did Peter, James, and John at the transfiguration, and as Paul did on the Damascus Road.

The lost sense of God's presence. When Samson violated his vow to God, he did not at first realize that the Lord had departed from him. Many of us have lost the sense of God's presence and anointing. We no longer minister in the power of the Holy Spirit. Our message has lost that certain something that is necessary for spiritual power.

The lost sensitivity to personal ethics. The Christian should be the most ethical person in our society. His income tax returns should be the most honest. The Christian minister should lean over backward in his honesty, truthfulness, and personal decorum. In the complexities of the present-day world, it is easy to get careless.

The lost simplicity of our love one to another. The one badge of Christian discipleship is not orthodoxy but love. There is far more emphasis on love and unity among God's people in the New Testament than there is on orthodoxy, as important as it is.

The lost significance of the scope of the church. We evangelicals sometimes set ourselves up as judges of another man's relationship to God. We often think that a person is not a Christian unless he pronounces our *shibboleths* and clichés exactly the way we do. I have found born-again Christians in the strangest places, under the oddest circumstances, who do not know our particular evangelical language. But their spirit witnesses to my spirit that they are truly sons of God. Labels such as *fundamentalist* and *liberal* do not always give a true reading of the heart.

The lost separation from the world. There is danger among evangelicals of compromising with the mode of the day. The lines of separation from the world are no longer drawn. Our attitudes are becoming infected with the spirit of the times. We are in danger of surrendering to false standards. While we must not be legalistic, we must be separated from the world. Worldliness is not a few designated things, such as materialism, movies, and money, but is a spirit that is invading our homes and our lives today through many other mediums. We need to issue a new call for separation, not only from the world, but unto God.

You may wonder what some of these things have to do with evangelism. They all have to do with Christians being committed to the Lord Jesus Christ. This personal commitment is the foundation of evangelism. We must be who we say we are before we can get the attention of those whom we want to win. Jesus said, "If ye love me, keep my commandments" (John 14:15). And he also said, "Thou shalt love the Lord thy God with all thy heart, and with all thy soul, and with all thy strength, and with all thy mind; and thy neighbour as thyself" (Luke 10:27). When we love God, we will keep his commandments. When we love our neighbor, we will have a passion to tell him of the Christ who can save his soul.

> *We must be who we say we are before we can get the attention of those whom we want to win.*

10

THE REVOLUTIONARY GOSPEL

Every few weeks we read in the headlines of another revolution somewhere in the world; an old regime has been overthrown and a new regime has taken over. Conversion is a revolution in the life of an individual. The old forces of sin, self-centeredness, and evil are overthrown from their place of supreme power. Jesus Christ is put on the throne.

No one can read the New Testament without recognizing that its message calls for conversion. Jesus said: "Except ye be converted . . . ye shall not enter into the kingdom of heaven" (Matthew 18:3). Paul encouraged men to be "reconciled to God" (2 Corinthians 5:20) and insisted that God now "commandeth all men everywhere to repent" (Acts 17:30). Paul viewed his office as that of an ambassador for Christ "as though God did beseech you by us" (2 Corinthians 5:20). It was

James who said: "Let him know, that he which converteth the sinner from the error of his way shall save a soul from death, and shall hide a multitude of sins" (James 5:20), and Peter taught that we are "born again, not of corruptible seed, but of incorruptible, by the word of God, which liveth and abideth forever" (1 Peter 1:23).

In reading the New Testament we are confronted with many incidents of men and women who encountered Christ either personally or through hearing the message preached. Something happened to them! None of their experiences were identical, but most of them experienced a change of mind and attitude and entered an entirely new dimension of living.

In my opinion there is no technical terminology for the biblical doctrine of conversion. Many words are used to describe or imply this experience; many biblical stories are used to illustrate it. I am convinced, however, after years of studying Scripture and observing conversions in the lives of thousands, that it is far more than a psychological phenomenon—it is the "turning" of the whole man to God.

PROCLAIMING THE BIBLE MESSAGE

I would suggest three elements which in combination I have found most effective in conversion. The first is the use of the Bible. The Bible needs more proclaiming than defending, and when proclaimed, its message can be relied upon to bring people to salvation. But it must be preached with a sense of authority. This is not authoritarianism or even dogmatism; it is preaching with utter confidence in the reliability of the *kerygma* (the original gospel that the apostles preached). A. M. Chirgwin observed that the Reformers "wanted everyone to have a chance to read the Bible because they believed profoundly in its converting power." This could be said of every great era of evangelism. I know of no great forward movements of the church of Jesus Christ that have not been closely bound up with the message of the Bible.

I remember when my attention was called to one of the most thrilling stories I have ever heard about the power of the Word of God. In 1941 an old Tzeltal Indian of southern Mexico approached a young man by the name of Bill Bentley in the village of Bachajon and said: "When I was north I heard of a book that tells about God. Do you know of such a book?" Bill Bentley did. In fact, he had a copy, he said; and if the tribe would permit him to build a house and live among them, he would translate the book into their language.

In the meantime, Bill returned to the United States to marry his fiancée, Mary Anna Slocum. Together they planned to go to Mexico in the fall. But when fall came, Mary Anna returned to Mexico alone. Six days before the wedding Bill had died suddenly, and Mary Anna had requested that the Wycliffe Bible Translators let her carry on his work. When she reached the village of Bachajon, the Indians had been warned against the white missionary, and instead of welcoming her, they threatened that if she settled among them, they would burn her house down. Settling in another part of the tribe, she began patiently to learn the Tzeltal language, translating portions of the Word of God and compiling a hymnbook in Tzeltal.

Six years passed and Mary Anna was joined by Florence Gerdel, a nurse. They started a clinic to which many Tzeltals came for treatment. Mary Anna had completed the translation of the Gospel of Mark and started on the book of Acts. A small chapel was built by the Indians who had abandoned their idols for the living Christ. In the highland village of Corralito, a little nucleus of believers grew from five families to seventy Christians, and they sent for the missionary women to come teach them the Word of God. Mary Anna and Florence went and were warmly welcomed by all seventy, who stood outside their huts and very reverently sang most of the hymns in the Tzeltal hymnbook. In little over a year there were four hundred believers. One of the most faithful was the former witch doctor, Thomas, who was among the first to throw his idols away.

By the end of the following year there were over one thousand believers. Because of the pressure of the crowds, Mary Anna could make little progress in her translation work. Concerned, the Indians freed the president of the congregation to help Mary Anna with the translation while they themselves took turns helping in his cornfield. When unbelieving Indians burned down their new chapel, the Christian Indians knelt in the smoldering ruins and prayed for their enemies. In the months following, many of these enemies were soundly converted to Christ.

By the end of 1958 there were more than five thousand Tzeltal believers in Corralito, Bachajon, and twenty other villages in the tribe. The New Testament in Tzeltal had been completed.

Mary Anna Slocum and another missionary moved to the Chol

tribe, where there was a small group of believers who desperately needed the Word of God in their own language. Others came to help. Indians volunteered to build the much-needed airstrip for the mission plane. As the believers multiplied, chapels large and small appeared throughout the area.

When the Chol New Testament was completed, there were over five thousand believers in that tribe and thirty congregations. One hundred young men had been trained to preach and teach, and a number had learned to do simple medical work. A missionary wrote:

> Formerly these Indians were indebted to the Mexican ranchers who lived in the area holding large coffee plantations. They also sold liquor. The Indians, before conversion, were habitual drunkards, in debt to these landholders. To pay off their debts the landowners forced them to work on their plantations whenever they needed work. After the Indians became Christians, they stopped their drinking, paid off their debts and began to plant their own coffee plantations. The coffee of the ranchers was left unharvested. As a result, the Mexican ranchers have been forced to sell the land to the Indians and are moving out of the area.

What a tremendous illustration of the power of the Scriptures! I am more convinced than ever that the Scriptures do not need to be defended but proclaimed.

A CHRIST-CENTERED THEOLOGY

The second element in effective evangelism is a clearly defined theology of evangelism—not so much a new theology but a special emphasis upon certain aspects of the theology that has been in the mainstream of the church throughout its history, both Catholic and Protestant. It is the theology that focuses attention upon the person and work of Christ on behalf of the alienated in every generation, the theology that invites sinful men to be reconciled to God.

Dr. D. T. Niles has written:

> No understanding of Christian evangelism is possible without an appreciation of the nature of Christian proclamation. It is not an affirmation of ideals which men must test and practice; it is not an explanation of life and its problems about which men may argue and with which in some form they must agree; it is rather the announcement of an event with which men must reckon. "God has made Him both Lord and Christ." There is a finality about that pronouncement. It is independent of human opinion and human choice.[1]

DEPENDENCE ON THE HOLY SPIRIT

The third element in effective evangelism is an awareness that conversion is a supernatural change brought about by the Holy Spirit, who himself communicates the truth. At every evangelistic conference we hear discussion of "how we can communicate the gospel to our age." We must always remember that the Holy Spirit is the communicating agent.

Without the work of the Holy Spirit there would be no such thing as conversion. The Scriptures teach that this is a supernatural work of God. It is the Holy Spirit who convicts men of sin. Jesus said: "And when he is come, he will reprove the world of sin, and of righteousness, and of judg-

> *Without the work of the Holy Spirit there would be no such thing as conversion.*

ment" (John 16:8). It is the Holy Spirit who gives new life. "Not by works of righteousness which we have done, but according to his mercy he saved us, by the washing of regeneration, and renewing of the Holy Ghost" (Titus 3:5).

There is a mystery in one aspect of conversion that I have never been able to fathom, and I have never read a book of theology that satisfies me at this point—the relation between the sovereignty of God and man's free will. It seems to me that both are taught in the Scriptures and both are involved. Certainly we are ordered to proclaim the gospel, and man is urged to respond.

This one act, however, is not the end of the matter. It is only the beginning! The Scriptures teach that the Holy Spirit comes to indwell each believing heart (1 Corinthians 3:16). It is the Holy Spirit who produces the fruit of the Spirit: love, joy, peace, longsuffering, gentleness, goodness, faith, meekness, temperance (Galatians 5:22–23). It is the Holy Spirit who guides us and enlightens us as we study the Scriptures (Luke 12:12). We are told that we can also be "filled" with the Spirit (Ephesians 5:18). The missionary expansion of the church in the early centuries was a result of the Great Commission (Matthew 28:19–20) and no less of the joyful constraint created in believers' hearts at Pentecost. The people had been filled with the Spirit. This great event was such a transforming experience that they did not need to refer to a prior command for their missionary activities. They were spontaneously moved to proclaim the gospel.

While there is no doubt that certain persons have a charismatic endowment by the Holy Spirit for evangelism (Ephesians 4:11), yet in a sense every Christian is to be an evangelist. In little more than ten years, Paul established churches in four provinces of the empire—Galatia, Macedonia, Achaia, and Asia. Before AD 47 there were no churches in these provinces. By AD 57 Paul could speak as if his work there was done and could plan extensive tours into the Far West without anxiety that the churches he had founded might perish in his absence. Such speed and thoroughness in the establishment of churches cannot be explained apart from the operation of the Holy Spirit and a sense of responsibility for evangelism by every Christian.

The missionary responsibility was interwoven with the most important offices of the early church. Each bishop was expected to be an evangelist and to encourage the evangelization of pagans in his own diocese. Some of the renowned missionaries of the postapostolic period were Gregory Thaumaturgus of Pontus, who became bishop in 240 and carried on successful evangelistic work in his diocese; Gregory the Illuminator of Armenia, under whom a mass conversion took place; Ulfilas, who preached to the Goths; the enthusiastic Martin of Tours; Ambrose of Milan; and Augustine of Hippo. Almost all of these people were converts to Christianity and propagated their newly found faith with a Spirit-filled zeal reminiscent of the apostolic age.

I believe that if our clergy today were filled with the Spirit and out among the people, even on street corners, proclaiming the gospel in the power of the Holy Spirit, a new day would dawn for the church. Paul said that in Corinth he did not use clever words or persuasive language. He said: "I determined not to know any thing among you, save Jesus Christ, and him crucified" (1 Corinthians 2:2). He knew that in the cross and resurrection there was power to change an individual and a society.

Conversion is the impact of the *kerygma* upon the whole man, convincing his intellect, warming his emotions, and causing his will to act with decision! I have no doubt that if every Christian in the world suddenly began proclaiming the gospel and winning others to an encounter with Jesus Christ, the effect upon our society would be revolutionary.

11

THE CRUCIAL IMPORTANCE
OF EVANGELISM

Our world is on fire, and man without God cannot control the flames. The demons of hell have been let loose. The fires of passion, greed, hate, and lust are sweeping the world. We seem to be plunging madly toward Armageddon. We live in the midst of crisis, danger, fear, and death. We sense that something is about to happen. We know that things cannot go on as they are.

The prospect of a world whose population is growing at a fantastic rate has inspired nightmares in world statesmen, sociologists, philosophers, and theologians. For example, the current population of the world is about seven billion and growing at the rate of one billion every thirteen years.[1] Scientists warn us of "pathological togetherness"—a world not only where disease and poverty stalk but where there are terrifying psychological problems and insoluble political problems.

The very pressure of the population explosion is bringing an increase in racial and religious tension throughout the world. Unless the supernatural love of God controls the hearts of men, we may be on the verge of a worldwide racial or religious war too horrible to contemplate. The population explosion is also increasing the ideological differences that separate men. The world indeed has become a neighborhood without being a brotherhood. Scientists, educators, and editors have become "evangelists," proclaiming the grim message of a bitter, cynical despair.

The pages of almost every newspaper and every book scream, "The harvest is ripe!" Never has the soil of the human heart and mind been better prepared. Never has the grain been thicker. Never have we had more effective instruments in our hands to help us gather the harvest. Yet at a time when the harvest is the ripest in history, the church is floundering in tragic confusion.

An official of the World Council of Churches told a group of us at Bossy, Switzerland, many years ago that if that group were to adopt a definition of evangelism, it would split the council. Deep theological differences make it almost impossible to form a definition of evangelism and to give authoritative biblical guidelines to the church. But if the church is to fulfill the Lord's commission in Matthew 28 to evangelize the world, we must come to a clear understanding of the evangelistic and missionary responsibilities of the church. To that end, I want to address the points of confusion I see concerning evangelism and offer a biblical solution.

THE MEANING OF EVANGELISM

First, there is confusion throughout the church about the very meaning of the word evangelism. Definitions are formed to fit personal tastes. Some think of evangelism simply as getting people to come to church. Others think it means getting people to conform to a pattern of religious belief and behavior similar to their own. Some new definitions of evangelism entirely omit the winning of men to a personal encounter with Jesus Christ. Their proponents look upon evangelism as social action only. The secretary of evangelism of one of the great American denominations said years ago: "The redemption of the world is not dependent upon the souls we win for Christ. . . . There cannot be individual salvation. . . . Salvation has more to do with the whole society than with the individual soul. . . . We must not be satisfied to win people one by one. . . . Contemporary evangelism is moving away from winning souls one by one to the evangelization of the structures of society."

We cannot accept this interpretation of evangelism. Evangelism has social implications, but its primary thrust is the winning of men and women to a personal relationship to Jesus Christ.

There has been a change in understanding of the nature and mission of the church, from "the church *has* a mission" to "the church *is* mission." There has been a change of emphasis from the spiritual nature of the church task to one of secular reformation. This new "evangelism" leads many to reject the idea of conversion in its historical biblical meaning and to substitute education and social reform for the work of the Holy Spirit in converting and changing people. All these ideas would have appalled our preachers and church leaders a century ago, not to mention the evangelists of the first century.

> *There has been a change of emphasis from the spiritual nature of the church task to one of secular reformation.*

The early Christians went by land and sea to spread the "evangel," the good news that God was in Christ, reconciling the world unto himself. This phenomenon of people claiming others for Christ is emphasized in the New Testament by the fact that the Greek word for "evangelize" is used fifty-two times and the noun form of "good news" or "gospel" is used seventy-four times. The early church proclaimed to the world: "We have found hope for despair, life for death, forgiveness for guilt, purpose for existence!" They shouted to the world, "We have found it, and having found it, we must share it!" That was the evangelism of the early church.

It seems to me that we cannot improve on the definition of evangelism that was given to us by the International Missionary Council at Madras in 1938: "Evangelism . . . must so present Christ Jesus in the power of the Holy Spirit, that men shall come to put their trust in God through him, to accept him as their Savior and serve him as their Lord in the fellowship of his church."

Evangelism means bearing witness, with the soul aflame, with the objective of winning men to a saving knowledge of the Lord Jesus Christ.

A lay evangelist once approached a woman in a Boston hotel and said: "Do you know Christ?" When she told her husband of this, he said: "Why didn't you tell him to mind his own business?" She said: "If you had seen the expression on his face, and heard the earnestness with which he spoke, you would have thought it was his business."

Oh, that God would give us a love for souls like that! Let us ask God to warm our hearts and set our souls on fire until we have a burning passion for the souls of men.

THE MOTIVE FOR EVANGELISM

There is not only confusion about the meaning of "evangelism"; there is also confusion about the motive for evangelism. There should never be any doubt that the commander-in-chief, the head of the church, *the Lord Jesus Christ, has given a command.* Failing to heed this command is deliberate disobedience. Three of the four Gospels end with a commission to the church to evangelize the world.

In Acts 1:8 we read: "You will receive power when the Holy Spirit has come upon you; and you shall be My witnesses in Jerusalem, and in all Judea and Samaria, and even to the remotest part of the earth" (NASB). At the end of the walk to Emmaus, which is also the climax of Luke's Gospel, the Lord, in opening the minds of his companions to understand the Scriptures, says: "Thus it is written, that the Christ would suffer and rise again from the dead the third day, and that repentance for forgiveness of sins would be proclaimed in His name to all the nations, beginning from Jerusalem" (Luke 24:46–47 NASB).

The command in Acts 1:8 is all-inclusive, embracing evangelism in all possible circumstances. "The remotest part of the earth" represents every conceivable situation—taking account of every possible language, race, color, and even religious belief. There was no syncretism here! There is an exclusiveness about the gospel that cannot be surrendered. If there were no other reason for going to the ends of the earth proclaiming the gospel and winning souls, the command of Christ would be enough! It is not optional. We are ambassadors under authority.

The second motive for evangelism is *the example of the preaching of the apostles.* An evangelistic objective was at the very heart and core of their preaching.

The third motive for evangelism should be that *the love of Christ constrains us,* as Paul said in 2 Corinthians 5:14. The most important thing that has ever happened to us as Christians is our acceptance of Christ as Lord and Savior. We immediately want to share it with others.

One of the greatest tragedies of our day is that so many professing Christians lack the desire to share their experience with others. Dr. James S. Stewart of Edinburgh has said: "The real problem of Christianity is not atheism or skepticism, but the non-witnessing Christian trying to smuggle his own soul into heaven."

The fourth motive for evangelism is the *approaching judgment.* The apostle Paul said: "Knowing therefore the terror of the Lord, we persuade men" (2 Corinthians 5:11). The background for the gospel of Jesus Christ is not only the love of God but also the wrath of God! In the solemn light of the day of judgment, man's greatest need is for reconciliation with God. Christ bore our sins on the cross in order that we, through faith in him, might be reconciled to God.

This brings us to one of the most important points of confusion in the mission of the church today: are men really lost? The great weight of modern theological opinion is against the fact that anyone is ultimately lost. The various shades of universalism prevalent throughout the church have done more to blunt evangelism and take the heart out of the missionary movement than anything else.

I believe the Scriptures teach that men outside of Jesus Christ are lost! There are many problems and many mysteries here, and I do not have time to go into the matter in detail. In Matthew 7:21–23, our Lord says to some men: "Depart from me." Here is final judgment! He said also: "He that believeth not is condemned already" (John 3:18). Language cannot get plainer than this! To me the doctrine of a future judgment, where men will be held accountable to God, is clearly taught in the Scriptures.

The fifth motive for evangelism is *the spiritual, social, and moral needs of men.* "Jesus had compassion on them" is a phrase used more than once in the Gospels. He looked upon men not only as souls separated from God by sin but also as sick bodies that needed his healing touch, empty stomachs that needed feeding, persons whose racial misunderstandings needed his Word (for example, his experience at Capernaum in Matthew 8 and his story of the Good Samaritan in Luke 10). Thus evangelism has a social responsibility.

The social, psychological, moral, and spiritual needs of others become a burning motivation for evangelism. I am convinced, however, that if the church went back to its main task of proclaiming the gospel and getting people converted to Christ, it would have a far greater impact on the social, moral, and psychological needs of people than it could achieve through any other thing it could possibly do. Some of the greatest social movements of history have come about as the result of men and women being converted to Christ. For example, the conversion of Wilberforce led to the freeing of slaves. Scores of current and up-to-date illustrations could be used. We have made the mistake of putting the cart before the horse. We are exhorting men to love each other before they have the capacity to love each other. This capacity can only come about through a personal relationship with Jesus Christ.

THE MESSAGE OF EVANGELISM

We have discussed the confusion about the meaning of and the motive for evangelism; but *there is also confusion about the message of evangelism.* More and more there is pressure to accommodate the Christian message to minds and hearts darkened by sin—to give precedence to material and physical needs while distorting the spiritual need that is basic to every person. This change in emphasis is really changing Christianity to a new humanism.

The great question today is: Is the first-century gospel relevant for the twenty-first century? Or has it as little to say to modern man as some radical theologians would have us believe?

The apostle Paul sums up the gospel in 1 Corinthians 15:1–4: "I declare unto you the gospel which I preached unto you, which also ye have received, and wherein ye stand; by which also ye are saved. . . . For I delivered unto you first of all that which I also received, how that Christ died for our sins according to the scriptures; and that he was buried, and that he rose again the third day according to the scriptures."

When Paul preached this message in Corinth, nothing seemed more irrelevant to the people of that day. However, the Holy Spirit took this message and transformed the lives of many in that city. Dr. James Stewart points out: "The driving force of the early Christian mission was not propaganda of beautiful ideals of the brotherhood of man. It was the proclamation of the mighty acts of God. At the heart of the apostles' message was the atoning sacrifice paid on Calvary."[2]

The apostle Paul himself said: "This doctrine of the cross is sheer folly to those on their way to ruin, but to us who are on the way to salvation it is the power of God. . . . God has made the wisdom of this world look foolish. As God in his wisdom ordained, the world failed to find him by its wisdom, and he chose to save those who have faith by the folly of the Gospel" (1 Corinthians 1:18–21 NEB). Thus the message of the gospel that we must proclaim to the world is: Christ died for our sins; he has been raised from the dead; you must be converted by turning from your sins and by putting your faith in Jesus Christ as Savior!

THE ENEMY OF EVANGELISM

There is confusion about the strategy of the enemy of evangelism. To Jesus and the apostles, Satan was very real. He was called "the prince of this world," "the god of this world," and "the prince of the power of the air." The names used for him indicate something of his character and strategy. He was called "deceiver," "liar," "murderer," "accuser," "tempter," "destroyer," and many other such names.

Satan's greatest strategy is deception. His most successful strategy has been to get modern theologians to deny his existence. The apostle Paul said, "Satan himself is transformed into an angel of light" (2 Corinthians 11:14).

When the seed of the gospel is being sown, Satan is always there sowing the tares. He also has the power to blind the minds of those whom we seek to evangelize: "The god of this world hath blinded the minds of them which believe not, lest the light of the glorious gospel of Christ, who is the image of God, should shine unto them" (2 Corinthians 4:4). His strategy is to use deception, force, evil, and error to destroy the effectiveness of the gospel. If we ignore the existence of Satan or are ignorant of his devices, then we fall into his clever trap.

However, we have the glorious promise that "greater is he that is in you, than he that is in the world" (1 John 4:4).

THE METHOD OF EVANGELISM

There is also confusion about the method of evangelism. Every nation in the world differs in its attitude toward Jesus Christ and its willingness to respond to the gospel. I found in my travels around the world, however, that while the approach may be different here and there, the spiritual needs of men are the same. I no longer spoke to laboring men as laboring men, to university students as university students, to Africans as Africans, to Americans as Americans. I spoke to all as men in need of redemption and salvation.

Evangelist Leighton Ford listed six methods of evangelism found in the New Testament:

> (1) *mass evangelism*—the kind of evangelism practiced by John the Baptist, Peter, Jesus, Stephen, and Paul; (2) *personal evangelism*—thirty-five personal interviews of Jesus alone are recorded in the Gospels; (3) *impromptu evangelism*—Jesus at the well, Peter and John at the Gate Beautiful; (4) *dialogue evangelism*—Paul at Mars Hill, Apollos at Ephesus (Acts 18:24); (5) *systematic evangelism*—the seventy sent out by Jesus two by two, the house-to-house visitation mentioned in Acts 5:42; and (6) *literary evangelism*—John 20:31

and Luke 1:1–4 give us clear statements of the evangelistic, apologetic intent of the writers of these Gospels.

No one method will be right for every person in every situation at every time, but some method of evangelism is certainly right for all people in all situations at all times! The Holy Spirit can take any method and use it to win souls.

Our goal is nothing less than the penetration of the entire world. Jesus said: "This gospel of the kingdom shall be preached in all the world for a witness unto all nations; and then shall the end come" (Matthew 24:14). Here evangelism is put into an eschatological context. We are not promised that the whole world will believe. The evangelization of the world does not mean that all people will respond but that all will be given an opportunity to respond as they are confronted with Christ.

Most of the illustrations of the gospel used by Jesus—salt, light, bread, water, leaven, fire—have one common element: penetration. Thus the Christian is true to his calling only when he is permeating the entire world. Not only are we to penetrate the world geographically; we are also to penetrate the worlds of government, school, work, and home, the worlds of entertainment, of the intellectual, of the laboring man, of the ignorant man.

The world desperately needs moral reform, and if we want moral reform, the quickest and surest way is by evangelism. The transforming gospel of Jesus Christ is the only possible way to reverse the moral trends of the present hour.

David Brainerd, in his journal of his life among the North American Indians, said: "I found that when my people were gripped by this great evangelical doctrine of Christ, and Him crucified, I had no need to give them instructions about morality. I found that one followed as sure and inevitable fruit of the other."[3]

Do we want social reform? The preaching of the cross and the Resurrection has been primarily responsible for promoting humanitarian sentiment and social concern for the past four hundred years. Prison reform, the prohibition of the slave trade, the abolition of slavery, the crusade for human dignity, the struggle against exploitation—all are the outcome of the great religious revivals and the conversion of individuals. The preaching of the cross could do more to bring about social revolution than any other method.

Do we want unity among Christians throughout the world? Then evangelize! I believe that some of the greatest demonstrations of ecumenicity in the world have been the evangelistic crusades where people by the thousands from various denominations have met to evangelize. We see a dedication, a zeal, and a spirit in these meetings not found in other gatherings.

Our greatest need, however, is *not* organizational union. Our greatest need is for the church to be baptized with the fire of the Holy Spirit and to go out proclaiming the gospel everywhere. We must first have spiritual unity in the gospel. Eight cylinders in a car are no better than four if there is no spark from the battery and no gas in the tank.

But one of the great questions is: can the church be revived in order to complete the penetration of the world in our generation?

The revival that the church so desperately needs cannot be organized and promoted by human means. It cannot be created by machinery. The two symbols of Pentecost were wind and fire. Both of these speak to us of the mystical, supernatural work of the Holy Spirit in revival. The meaning of the word "revive" in the Old Testament is "to recover," "to restore," "to return" to God's standard for his people. The word for "revive" in the New Testament means "to stir up" or "to rekindle a fire that is slowly dying."

The Christian continually feels the pull of the world, the flesh, and the devil. This is why Paul exhorted young Timothy to "fan into flame the gift of God" (2 Timothy 1:6 NIV). Even the members of the early church needed fresh renewing. In chapter two of Acts we find that the believers were filled with the Holy Spirit in the upper room; yet in chapter four we read of their being filled once again: "And when they had prayed, the place was shaken where they were assembled together; and they were all filled with the Holy Ghost, and they spake the word of God with boldness" (Acts 4:31).

In my travels around the world I met many sincere Christian leaders who believed that it is impossible to have a worldwide revival. They based their assertions on the prediction in Scripture that "in the last days perilous times shall come," when there will be a wholesale departure from the faith (2 Timothy 3:1). They admitted that the gospel has lost none of its ancient power to save and that here and there a few souls will be gathered in. But they believed that there will be no outpourings of the Holy Spirit before the end of the age. They argued that it is completely out of the plans and purposes of God for the church to pray for and expect a mighty revival.

Brethren, I do not believe that the day of miracles has passed. As long as the Holy Spirit abides and works on the earth, the church's potential is the same as it was in the apostolic days. The great Paraclete—the Holy Spirit—has never been withdrawn, and he still waits to work through those who are willing to meet his conditions of repentance, humility, and obedience.

I am convinced that God could touch the world in our generation. If we will meet God's conditions, he will send us a time of refreshing, revival, and awakening.

After fifteen years in China, Jonathan Goforth came to the deep and painful conviction that God had something mightier to do in his life and ministry. He became restless as he began, under the Spirit's anointing, an intense study of the Scriptures in relation to revival. After months of study and prayer, he began to believe that God would fulfill his Word in the most difficult field in the world. That was the beginning of the great Manchurian revival.

Henry Martyn once wrote: "If ever I see a Hindu a real believer in the Lord Jesus, I shall see something more nearly approaching the resurrection of a dead body than anything I have yet seen."[4] But Martyn carried on in faith, believing the promises of God, and lived to see the day when God began to work among the Hindus.

We are tempted at times to cry with Habakkuk, "O Lord, how long shall I cry, and thou wilt not hear!" (Habakkuk 1:2). The prophet was discouraged as he saw the overwhelming odds against the work of the Lord. He had almost reached the point of despair. God gave him a glorious answer: "I will work a work in your days which ye will not believe, though it be told you" (1:5). In other words, God was saying to his despondent prophet: "If I told you what I am doing in the world, you wouldn't believe it."

All humanity is composed of different racial, linguistic, and cultural backgrounds—but before God with our spiritual needs, we are one race! We have only one gospel to declare in every generation, and that is, "God was in Christ, reconciling the world unto himself" (2 Corinthians 5:19). We have one task—the penetration of the entire world in our generation with the gospel! God, help us to better understand and do our task.

12

WHY THE WORD
MATTERS SO MUCH

It is a sultry day with a hot breeze spinning little dust whirls down the winding road by the Sea of Galilee. There is an air of expectancy everywhere. We hear voices, raised to an excited pitch as friend calls a greeting to friend. Down every trail leading to Galilee, little clusters of people make their way. Word has spread abroad that Jesus is returning to Galilee.

Suddenly he and his little band of followers come over the brow of a little hill on the Capernaum road. Following close behind swarms a vast multitude of people from Decapolis, Jerusalem, Judea, and beyond Jordan.

Quickly the word passes from mouth to mouth: "Jesus is coming." Crowds from Bethsaida and Capernaum soon appear and join the others. Together they follow the little band of thirteen men, simply dressed in flowing robes. As they reach the summit of the hill, where gentle winds afford relief from the heat, Jesus stops and motions for all to sit down and rest. The air is tense. It is a moment to be captured and held for eternity. The crowd hushes as Jesus mounts a large rock and sits down. Quiet falls upon the multitude, their faces turned expectantly toward Jesus. Then he moves his lips and begins to speak.

What he was saying there, on that "Mount of Beatitudes" in far-away Palestine, was to illuminate the pages of history. The most profound, the most sublime words ever uttered were spoken there that day. In simple words, Jesus revealed to his dumbfounded hearers the inner depth of God's commandments and a new way of life!

No one who once heard Jesus could ever again be the same. What was the secret of this master teacher? How did he hold those crowds spellbound?

"And it came to pass, when Jesus had ended these sayings, the people were astonished at his doctrine: for he taught them as one *having authority*" (Matthew 7:28–29, emphasis added). Is not this authoritative note part of the secret of the earthly ministry of Christ?

The Prophets and the Revelation

The great prophets of the past had also spoken with authority. The impact of their preaching cannot be traced simply to an authoritative technique. Nor was their authoritative note based on confidence merely in the rightness of their own intentions and speculations. Their secret is traceable to nothing less than the confidence that they were the mediators of divine revelation. Throughout the Old Testament we find Isaiah, Jeremiah, Hosea, and the other prophets continually using such expressions as "The word of the Lord came unto me" or "Thus saith the Lord." The flaming prophets of old gained their authority from this: they were not simply speaking their own words; they were mouthpieces for God.

The authority of Jesus is more than a prophetic authority. The Christian church rightly acknowledges that in him alone the incarnate God entered history; the very words he spoke are the words of the one and only God-man. Yet the remarkable fact is that in his teachings Jesus continually referred to passages in the Old Testament as fully authoritative. His messianic self-consciousness, his very authority as the Son of God, are combined with the highest regard for the Old Testament as the authoritative record of the will of God.

Even a casual study of church history will reveal that the great giants of pulpit and pen, from Augustine to Wesley, relied heavily on Scripture for their authority. In doing this, they followed a sacred precedent hallowed by Christ and the apostles.

MY BATTLE WITH DOUBT

In 1949 I had been having a great many doubts concerning the Bible. I thought I saw apparent contradictions in Scripture. Some things I could not reconcile with my restricted concept of God. When I stood up to preach, the authoritative note so characteristic of all great preachers of the past was lacking. Like hundreds of other young seminary students, I was waging the intellectual battle of my life. The outcome could certainly affect my future ministry.

In August of that year I had been invited to Forest Home, a Presbyterian conference center high in the mountains outside Los Angeles. I remember walking down a trail, tramping into the woods, and almost wrestling with God. I dueled with my doubts, and my soul seemed to be caught in the crossfire. Finally, in desperation, I surrendered my will to the living God revealed in Scripture. I knelt before the open Bible and said: "Lord, many things in this Book I do not understand. But thou hast said, 'The just shall live by faith.' All I have received from thee, I have taken by faith. Here and now, by faith, I accept the Bible as thy word. I take it all. I take it without reservations. Where there are things I cannot understand, I will reserve judgment until I receive more light. If this pleases thee, give me authority as I proclaim thy Word, and through that authority convict me of sin and turn sinners to the Savior."

PREACHING FROM THE BIBLE

Within six weeks we started our Los Angeles crusade. During that crusade I discovered the secret that changed my ministry. I stopped trying to prove that the Bible was true. I had settled in my own mind that it was, and this faith was conveyed to the audience. Over and over again I found myself saying, "The Bible says." I felt as though I were merely a voice through which the Holy Spirit was speaking.

Authority created faith. Faith generated response, and hundreds of people were compelled to come to Christ. A crusade scheduled for three weeks lengthened into eight weeks, with hundreds of thousands of people in attendance. The people were not coming to hear great oratory, nor were they interested merely in my ideas. I found they were desperately hungry to hear what God had to say through his Holy Word.

I felt as though I had a rapier in my hand and, through the power of the Bible, was slashing deeply into men's consciences, leading them to surrender to God. Does not the Bible say of itself, "For the word of God is quick, and powerful, and sharper than any twoedged sword, piercing even to the dividing asunder of soul and spirit, and of the joints and marrow, and is a discerner of the thoughts and intents of the heart" (Hebrews 4:12)?

I found that the Bible became a flame in my hands. That flame melted away unbelief in the hearts of the people and moved them to decide for Christ. The Word became a hammer breaking up stony hearts and shaping them into the likeness of God. Did not God say, "I will make my words in thy mouth fire" (Jeremiah 5:14) and "Is not my word like as a fire? . . . and like a hammer that breaketh the rock in pieces" (Jeremiah 23:29)?

I found that I could take a simple outline and put a number of pertinent Scripture quotations under each point, and God would use this mightily to cause men to make full commitment to Christ. I found that I did not have to rely upon cleverness, oratory, psychological manipulation of crowds, apt illustrations, or striking quotations from famous men. I began to rely more and more upon Scripture itself, and God blessed.

HUNGER FOR GOD'S WORD

I am convinced, through my travels and experiences, that people all over the world are hungry to hear the Word of God. As the people came to a desert place to hear John the Baptist proclaim, "Thus saith the Lord," so modern man in his confusions, frustrations, and bewilderments will come to hear the minister who preaches with authority.

I remember how in London many secular and religious journalists remarked on this very point as being perhaps the greatest secret of the meetings there in 1954. One of the thousands who came to commit their lives to Christ in that crusade was a brilliant young communist. She was a student at the Royal Academy of Drama and Arts, and was already a successful young actress. She had joined the Young Communist League because the members were zealous and seemed to have the answers to the problems of life. Out of curiosity she and some of her fellow students came to our meetings at the Harringay Arena "to see the show." She later testified how startled she was to hear not a lecture on sociology, politics, psychology, or philosophy, but the simple Word of God quoted. This fascinated her and her companions. They came back several nights until the Word of God did its work of breaking open their hearts. They surrendered their lives to Christ.

THE BUGABOO OF BIBLIOLATRY

I am not advocating bibliolatry. I am not suggesting that we should worship the Bible, any more than a soldier worships his sword or a surgeon worships his scalpel. I am, however, fervently urging a return to Bible-centered preaching, a gospel presentation that says without apology and without ambiguity, "Thus saith the Lord."

The world longs for authority, finality, and conclusiveness. It is weary of theological floundering and uncertainty. Belief exhilarates the human spirit; doubt depresses. Nothing is gained psychologically or spiritually by casting aspersions on the Bible. A generation that occupied itself with criticism of the Scriptures all too soon found itself questioning divine revelation.

> *Belief exhilarates the human spirit; doubt depresses.*

It is my conviction that if the preaching of the gospel is to be authoritative, if it is to produce conviction of sin, if it is to challenge men and women to walk in newness of life, if it is to be attended by the Spirit's power, then the Bible with its discerning, piercing, burning message must become the basis of our preaching.

From my experience in preaching across America, I am convinced that the average American is vulnerable to the Christian message if it is seasoned with authority and proclaimed as truly from God through his Word.

Do we not have authority in other realms of life? Mathematics has its inviolable rules, formulas, and equations; if these are ignored, no provable answers can be found.

Music has its rules of harmony, progression, and time. The greatest music of the ages has been composed in accordance with these rules. To break the rules is to produce discord and "audio-bedlam." The composer uses imagination and creative genius, to be sure, but his work must be done within the framework of the accepted forms of time, melody, and harmony. He must go by the book. To ignore the laws of music would be to make no music.

Every intelligent action takes place in a climate of authority.

THE AUTHORITY FOR BASIC TRUTH

I use the phrase "the Bible says" because the Word of God is the authoritative basis of our faith. I do not continually distinguish between the authority of God and the authority of the Bible because I am confident that he has made his will known authoritatively in the Scriptures.

If God's will is so clearly revealed, why do so many Christians and churches disagree about it? The world is more than a little weary of our doubts and our conflicting opinions and views. But I have discovered that there is much common ground in the Bible—broad acres of it—upon which most churches can agree. Could anything be more basic than the acknowledgment of sin, the atonement, man's need of repentance and forgiveness, the prospect of immortality, and the dangers of spiritual neglect?

There need be no adulteration of truth or compromise on the great biblical doctrines. I think it was Goethe who said, after hearing a young minister, "When I go to hear a preacher preach, I may not agree with what he says, but I want him to believe it." Even a vacillating unbeliever has no respect for the man who lacks the courage to preach what he believes.

MESSENGERS AND THE MESSAGE

Very little originality is permitted a United Nations translator. His sole obligation is to convey the message he receives from the speaker to the persons who depend on him to deliver it in a language they can understand. He may not like to translate that message—it may contain bad news or present a policy that will distress those who hear it. But a responsible translator will not dare to change the message of the speaker. His duty is simply to convey the message to others.

We Christian ministers have the Word of God. Our commander said, "Go, take this message to a dying world!" Some ministers today neglect it; some tear up the message and substitute one of their own. Some delete part of it. Some tell the people that the Lord does not mean what he says. Others say that he really did not give the message, but that it was written by ordinary men who were all too prone to make mistakes.

Let us remember that we are sowing God's seed. Some indeed may fall on beaten paths and some among thorns, but it is our business to keep on sowing. We are not to stop sowing because some of the soil looks unpromising.

KEEP ON KEEPING ON

We are holding a light, and we are to let it shine. Though it may seem but a twinkling candle in a world of blackness, it is our business to let it shine.

We are blowing a trumpet. In the din and noise of battle the sound of our little trumpet may seem to be lost, but we must keep sounding the alarm to those in danger.

We are kindling a fire in this cold world full of hatred and selfishness. Our little blaze may seem to have no effect, but we must keep our fire burning.

We are striking with a hammer. The blows may seem only to jar our hands as we strike, but we are to keep on hammering.

We are wielding a sword. The first or second thrust may be parried, and all our efforts to strike deep into the enemy flank may seem hopeless. But we are to keep on attacking.

We have bread for a hungry world. The people may seem to be

feeding busily on other things, ignoring the Bread of Life, but we must keep on offering it to the souls of men.

We have water for parched souls. We must keep standing and crying out, "Ho, every one that thirsteth, come ye to the waters" (Isaiah 55:1).

Give a new centrality to the Bible in your own preaching. Jesus promised that much seed will find good soil and spring up and bear fruit. The fire in your heart and on your lips can kindle a sacred flame in some cold hearts and win them to Christ. The hammer will break some hard hearts and make them yield to God in contrition. The sword will pierce the armor of sin and cut away self-satisfaction and pride, and open man's heart to the Spirit of God. Some hungry men and women will take the Bread of Life and some thirsting souls will find the Water of Life. Preach the Scriptures with authority! You will witness a climactic change in your ministry.

13

MAXIMIZING THE MESSAGE AND THE METHOD

Early in my ministry I was in Dallas, Texas, and we had a crowd of thirty thousand to forty thousand people. I preached and gave an invitation and practically no one came forward. I left the platform a little bit perplexed and wondering what had happened. A saint from Germany put his arm around me and said, "Billy, could I say a word to you?" I said, "Yes." He said, "Son, you didn't preach the cross tonight. Your message was good, but you didn't preach the cross." I went to my room and wept. I said, "O God, so help me, there will never be a sermon that I preach unless the cross is central."

Now, there are many mysteries to the atonement, and I don't understand all the light that comes from that cross. But to lift it up is the secret of evangelistic preaching.

RESPONSE TO THE CROSS

Evangelism must seek the response of the individual. A lady said to me some time ago, "You know, Mr. Graham, our minister is a wonderful person, but for the life of me, I don't know what he wants us to do." There are many people like that. Are we failing to explain those things that to us are elementary? What is repentance? How long has it been since you preached a sermon on repentance just as you would explain it to a group of children? Dr. Louis Evans, one of our great Presbyterian ministers, said that in his preaching he found that the religious intelligence of the average American congregation is that of a twelve-year-old. "I always talk to the people now as if they were children," he added. Dr. James Denney once said, "If you shoot over the head of your congregation, you don't prove anything except that you don't know how to shoot."

I've found that there is something powerful about using the language God used. And I go back to words like *repentance* and *faith* and the *blood.* Somehow the Holy Spirit makes it plain in simple terminology. That is what Christ did. When Christ preached, William Barclay says, he took his illustrations on the spur of the moment. He did not sit in a study and think them out. One day he saw a fig tree and used it as an illustration.

We make it so complicated. Jesus explained things so simply that the common people heard him gladly. Of course, the Pharisees missed it. The intellectuals failed to grasp what he was talking about. Many times the condition of our hearts governs the receiving of the message as much as does the explanation.

I think that the evangelist must recognize that many factors lead to a person's commitment to Christ. I would go so far as to say I do not think I have ever led a soul to Christ. A pastor's sermon, a mother's prayer, an incident in battle—all these contribute to a process toward conversion. And those who were converted in our evangelistic meetings were not converted by the preaching of Billy Graham. I was just one in a series of many factors that brought people to this giving of themselves to the Savior.

People come in different ways. Lydia was led by her emotions, the Philippian jailer by his will, Paul by his conscience, and Cornelius by his intellect. I certainly do not say that all come the same way.

It seems to me that evangelism must avoid over-emotion. Years ago I found that I could work on the emotions of the congregation and get people to respond, but without tears of repentance. They were tears of a superficial emotion. People come to Christ by hearing the Word of God. Emotion, however, does have its place. You cannot imagine two young people in love kissing each other out of a cold sense of duty. And the evangelist cannot offer free pardon for sinners and forbid any reaction of joy.

The dread of emotion in religious experience has gone to extreme lengths. W. E. Sangster has said: "Some critics appear to suspect any conversion which does not take place in a refrigerator." In his little book *Let Me Commend,* he goes on to say that "the man who screams at a football or baseball game, but is distressed when he hears of a sinner weeping at the Cross and murmurs something about the dangers of emotionalism hardly merits intelligent respect."[1] Folks can sit in front of a television and watch a popular sitcom or a tense police drama and laugh or bite their fingernails off. But if there is any joy or tear or smile over religion—then we are to watch out for emotion. That is one of the devil's biggest laughs.

Extending the Invitation

Many people ask, why give a public invitation? This was a stumbling block to me for a while, I must confess. And I would like to acknowledge in passing that so-called "mass evangelism" has deficits and assets. One deficit is this: people go to the meetings, they hear the beautiful singing, they are wonderfully lifted up in spirit, the preacher stands up and shouts and pounds the pulpit—and then they go back to their own church service and wonder why it is not the same.

I explain carefully in my preaching that the worship service is more important than the evangelistic service. The holiest moment is when we come to the Communion table, for that is worship of God; it is his church at worship. Ours is an evangelistic service designed to reach those outside the church as well as those on the fringe of the church. These are two different things, and the worship service is most important.

Nonetheless, it might do the people good if ministers started pounding the pulpit a bit. A lady said to me in San Francisco: "Mr. Graham, you know my preacher is preaching new sermons since you came. You really helped him." I said, "Madam, did you come forward?" She said, "Oh, yes." I said, "Could it be that you are listening with different ears, and that he's preaching the same sermons?" She said, "I hadn't thought about that. That may be."

Moses gave an invitation in Exodus 32:26 when he said, "Who is on the Lord's side? let him come unto me." That was a public invitation. Joshua gave an invitation: "Choose you this day whom ye will serve" (Joshua 24:15). King Josiah gave a public invitation when he called on the assembly of the people, after the book of the law had been found and read to them, to stand in assent to the keeping of the law (2 Chronicles 34:31–32). Ezra called upon the people to swear publicly to carry out his reformation (Ezra 10:5).

Jesus gave many public invitations. He said to Peter and Andrew, "Follow me, and I will make you fishers of men" (Matthew 4:19). He said to Matthew, "Follow me," and Matthew rose and followed him (Matthew 9:9). Jesus invited Zacchaeus publicly to come down out of the tree. "Zacchaeus, make haste, and come down; for to day I must abide at thy house" (Luke 19:5). Jesus told the parable of the slighted dinner invitation where the lord said to his servant: "Go out into the highways and hedges, and compel them to come in, that my house may be filled" (Luke 14:23). The apostles also gave invitations.

THE INQUIRY ROOM

The method of invitation we use is of comparatively recent origin, but the spirit and principle of the evangelistic invitation is, in my opinion, as old as the Bible itself. George Whitefield and John Wesley used to give public invitations, as did most of the evangelists. However, the modern inquiry room that we use with personal counseling (we coined the term "counseling" instead of personal workers) was not used so far as I can discover until 1817 when Ashland Middleton began using it. D. L. Moody made it popular and used it continually in his meetings; and when he gave an invitation, he would ask people to make their way not to the front but straight to a room. There he would go and speak to them all.

Now, we found that the weakest aspect of mass evangelism was at this point. How to overcome it was the problem. How could we get people to make a profession or indicate their spiritual need and do it properly so that each one would be dealt with personally? In other words, mass evangelism was only a stage for personal evangelism.

And so we began to teach and train counselors to talk to each individual. Some of the people who come forward at crusades are these "finders," but not all. Most of them are still seekers. They are inquiring; they are seeking help. They need someone to guide them, lead them, and direct them. You say that only the minister can do that. The early church was made up of laymen, and I believe that too long we have had a gap between the laity and the clergy. Laymen ought to be in the work of evangelism. That makes for the most successful church.

Dean Barton Babbage told me that in the cathedral in Melbourne he started what he calls "desk night" once a month. Members of the congregation go out and bring in unchurched people. On the first "desk night," he gave a public invitation and over three hundred people in the cathedral came forward! These people who were trained in the counseling classes cannot stop, he said. They are bringing evangelism back into the churches. Ministers ought to be prepared for this, for it will be one of the results.

At our crusades, our trained counselors write on a card the name and church preference of each seeker who comes forward. Then we send the card immediately to that church for follow-up. I remember the first time I went to Lambeth Palace to see the archbishop of Canterbury; he told me a little story. He said, "You know, we have a little chapel here at Lambeth, and two cards came (from the Harringay meetings) and somehow they were sent to me. I took them immediately, because if you don't, the Graham organization is going to send those cards to a Baptist church!"

THE LOSS OF BABES

Suppose we treated newborn babies as carelessly as we treat new Christians. The infant mortality rate would be appalling. Here is a little baby coming into my home, and I would say: "Son, we're so glad to have you in our home. Now, we hope you come around next Sunday; we're going to give you a good dinner. It won't last but an hour—but do come. See you next Sunday." He would die! And yet here are persons who come to Christ as spiritual babes, and we expect them to come to church all by themselves on Sunday mornings and get enough food to last them until the next Sunday when they can come back for more. That is not God's way at all! These people need help, guidance, leadership, and training in the study of the Word of God. I cannot possibly instruct all of them. I have them for one evening, and somehow the minister feels that the evangelist is to work miracles—that a new convert comes into the church a mature Christian, and if he should make one false move, in ignorance or in weakness, the church points the finger and says, "Uh-huh, a convert that didn't last!"

How pharisaical can we get? A beachhead has been established in their lives. Now it is up to us to follow through with an infantry attack. The crusades can establish beachheads in thousands of lives. But it is up to the laymen of the church to follow through with the people. They need our help. They are spiritual babies. The obstetrician must be followed by the pediatrician.

I trust that as you preach, you will make your sermons heartwarming and evangelistic. Take some of the old subjects like the new birth, repentance, faith, and justification, and see what happens. You say, "But my people are already far beyond that!" I do not believe that your Christian people are going to bring the unconverted into the church unless they think a simple gospel will be presented.

May I emphasize this important fact, however: a church's spiritual life will never rise any higher than the personal life of its people. I pray that to all Christians will come a new spirit for Christ, a new consecration and dedication. One of the great Anglican leaders in Australia called me to his home, closed the door, and locked it. He said to me, "I've been an Anglican priest for many years," and then he started weeping: "I need a new experience of God." We got on our knees and we prayed together.

Do you need a new experience with God, a new encounter with the living Christ? I pray that you will not be like Samson when he got up and did not realize the Lord had departed from him. Have you done it the same old way until you are almost a perfectionist, but have lost the compassion, love, burden, and vision of the living Christ? Pray that it might return—and with a double portion of his Spirit.

Part Three
GUARD YOURSELF

14

AVOIDING THE TRAPS
OF CELEBRITY

By William Martin

William Martin is the Harry and Hazel Chavanne Emeritus Professor of Religion and Public Policy in the Department of Sociology at Rice University. He is also the author of A Prophet with Honor: The Billy Graham Story, *a 1991 biography, based on hundreds of interviews, that is widely regarded as the most authoritative account of Graham's life. An updated edition of the book is forthcoming.*

O n countless occasions during his career, usually at a press conference preceding a major crusade, Billy Graham declared that he sensed religious revival was breaking out and about to sweep over the land. In 1948, he happened to be right. During the 1940s, church membership in America rose by nearly 40 percent, with most of the growth coming after the end of the war, when the nation tried to reconstruct normalcy on the most dependable foundation it knew. Church building reached an all-time high, seminaries were packed and secular colleges added programs in religious studies, religious books outsold all other categories of nonfiction, and Bible sales doubled between 1947 and 1952—the new Revised Standard Version of the Bible sold two million copies in 1950 alone. While Graham and his colleagues in Youth for Christ and the Southern Baptist "Youth Revival Movement" were packing civic auditoriums and stadiums, William Branham, Jack Coe, A. A. Allen, and Oral Roberts were filling stupendous nine-pole circus tents with Pentecostal believers desperate to see afflictions healed, devils cast out, and the dead raised.

AVOIDING THE SNARES OF SEX, MONEY, AND POWER

For evangelists, it was like being a stockbroker in a runaway bull market. As in other fields, however, the boom attracted some whose motives and methods were less than sanctified, who fell prey to the temptations described in Scripture as "the lust of the flesh, and the lust of the eyes, and the pride of life" (1 John 2:16), but better known by their street names, "sex, money, and power." Despite good intentions and behavior, Graham and his associates occasionally found themselves the objects of suspicion and condescension from ministers and laypeople alike. They learned that Elmer Gantry, whom Sinclair Lewis had assembled from skeletons and scraps found in the closets of real-life evangelists, was a deeply entrenched cultural stereotype.

As they contemplated the checkered history and contemporary shortcomings of itinerant evangelism (the term itself had a kind of siding-salesman's rhinestone ring to it) and talked with veteran campaigners, they realized that much of the skepticism was warranted. To prepare his own defenses, Graham called the members of his evangelistic team—George Beverly Shea, Grady Wilson, and Cliff Barrows—to his hotel room during a campaign in Modesto, California, in November 1948. "God has brought us to this point," he said. "Maybe he is preparing us for something that we don't know. Let's try to recall all the things that have been a stumbling-block and a hindrance to evangelists in years past, and let's come back together in an hour and talk about them and pray about them and ask God to guard us from them."

The assignment was easy. They had all seen enough evangelists rise and fall, or leave town in a cloud of disillusionment, to be able to pinpoint the key problems readily. When they regrouped in Graham's room later in the afternoon, each had made essentially the same list, which came to be known in the oral tradition as "The Modesto Manifesto."

The first problem was money. Some evangelists had deliberately worn their oldest suits during revivals or told gripping stories of sick children or lamented the broken-down condition of their homes or the high costs of transportation, and even the most rectitudinous of men could find it difficult not to pull out a few extra flourishes when the love offering was collected, typically on the last night of a revival. When he traveled for Youth for Christ, Graham turned offerings over to local or national bodies and was paid a straight salary. But no parent body existed to fund his independent revivals, so the group saw no viable alternative to the love-offering system, even though it made them uncomfortable. They did, however, pledge not to emphasize the offering and to try to keep themselves as free as possible of suspicion regarding the way they handled the money, by asking members of the sponsoring committee to oversee the payment of all bills and disbursement of funds to the revival team. On one occasion, Bev Shea sent the sponsoring committee a check for thirty dollars, just in case the hotel had levied a charge for extra laundry service for his infant son.

Two years after Modesto, Graham encountered an incident that spurred another change in financial arrangements. Billy Graham's 1950 Atlanta crusade, though a huge success, produced a major embarrassment for the evangelist. Though Graham had not sought it, the crusade committee had taken up a substantial "love offering" for him and his team at the closing service. The next day, the *Atlanta Constitution* ran photos of the collection, which then appeared in newspapers throughout the country, implying that Billy Graham, like itinerant evangelists before him, was demonstrating that one could serve both God and mammon.

Deeply stung, Graham determined to put all trace of the Elmer Gantry image behind him and asked Jesse Bader, secretary for evangelism at the National Council of Churches, for advice. Bader advised him to have the Billy Graham Evangelistic Association put him and his team on fixed salaries, unrelated to the number of crusades they might hold in a given year. Graham agreed and pegged his own salary at $15,000, comparable to that received by prominent urban pastors at the time, but less than he could have made from love offerings. He would later accept money for his newspaper column and royalties from some of his books, but never—after the system took effect in January 1952—would he or his team accept another honorarium for their work in a crusade.

The second potential problem was "immorality." As energetic young men in full bloom—often traveling without their families, charged with the raw excitement of standing before large and admiring crowds, and living in anonymous hotels and tourist courts—all of them knew well the power and possibilities of sexual temptation, and all of them had seen promising ministerial careers shipwrecked by the potent combination of lust and opportunity. They asked God "to guard us, to keep us true, to really help us be sensitive in this area, to keep us even from the appearance of evil," and they began to follow simple but effective rules to protect themselves. They avoided situations that would put them alone with a woman—lunch, a counseling session, even a ride to an auditorium or an airport. On the road, they roomed in close proximity to each other, as an added margin of social control. And always, they prayed for supernatural assistance in keeping themselves "clean."

Two other problems, less imperious in their prodding than

money or sex but capable of generating cynicism toward evangelists, were inflated publicity and criticism of local pastors. Because it helped win invitations to bigger churches and cities, and thus fed their egos and fattened their pocketbooks, evangelists had grown accustomed to exaggerating their crowds and their results, both in advance publicity and in reports to evangelical publications. Critics accused them of counting arms and legs instead of heads, and the phrase "evangelistically speaking" signified that anyone interested in accuracy should discount an itinerant's reports of his own accomplishments.

D. L. Moody refused to keep statistics, lest he be drawn into exaggeration or boasting. Billy Graham and his team were too wed to the modern ethos to adopt that approach, but they did begin to use a consistent procedure. Instead of generating their own figures, they usually accepted crowd estimates given by police or the fire department or arena managers, even when they felt the official estimate was too low, and they readily admitted that many who came down the aisles during the invitation were counselors assigned to help inquirers, not inquirers themselves.

As for the criticism of pastors, they had heard many a fire-breathing evangelist attack the local clergy to gain attention and make himself look good, then leave town while the hapless pastors tried to regain the confidence of their parishioners. Graham was determined to avoid this destructive course. He would gladly meet with pastors who criticized him but would not publicly criticize men who planted the seed and tilled the fields that he swooped in to harvest.

In addition to these major issues, the Graham team also pledged to avoid sensationalism, excessive emotionalism, anti-intellectualism, overemphasis on biblical prophecy or other controversial topics, and lack of proper follow-up on inquirers. There may have been others; no one kept a copy of the list, but the problems were so familiar that no one needed to.

THE EFFECTIVENESS OF THE MANIFESTO

Over the years, Graham and members of his team spoke of the Modesto Manifesto from time to time, often in response to inquiries from journalists about how he and his organization had managed to avoid scandal throughout decades of public ministry. It drew particular attention in the late 1980s, when sex and money scandals wrecked the ministries of Jim and Tammy Faye Bakker and Jimmy Swaggart, and Oral Roberts drew ridicule by claiming that God had threatened to end his life if his supporters didn't come up with $8 million in ransom money.

By coincidence, I happened to be spending several days with Mr. Graham at the time the Bakker scandals broke, as part of my research for my biography of Graham, *A Prophet with Honor.* He told me that reporters were calling from the broadcasting networks and major press outlets, urging him to comment, but that he was reluctant to talk to them. "If I say they should have taken the same measures we did to protect ourselves," he said, "I'll sound self-righteous, and I don't want to do that." It was clear, however, that he was once again grateful for having had the foresight to protect himself from this sort of debacle.

Graham's commitment to the financial principles of the Manifesto was demonstrated in 1977, when the *Charlotte Observer*, in an extensive story about the finances of the Billy Graham Evangelistic Association, charged that, while purporting to provide a full disclosure of its finances, the association had failed to reveal the existence of a fund containing assets worth nearly $23 million, perhaps because it feared such a revelation would make it difficult to keep asking supporters for donations. In fact, the creation of the fund in 1972 had been announced at a press conference and major media had mentioned it during the first year or two of its existence. Its stated purposes were to provide support for various evangelistic organizations such as Campus Crusade, to establish an evangelism institute at Wheaton, and to develop a layman's training center near Asheville. Any disbursement of its funds had been carefully documented and reported to the IRS. Legally, the fund was separate from BGEA and was incorporated in Texas, but its assets came from BGEA and its board was essentially identical to that of BGEA.

When the relevant history and facts were laid out, the cloud over the organization lifted, but the negative publicity and temporary drop in contributions made an impression on Billy Graham. Years later he told me, "We should have said, 'We've got another fund down in Texas that we are going to do thus and such with.' We told the government about it, but we didn't think the newspapers necessarily had a legitimate right to know about everything. I've changed my mind on

that. I think they do. Because I think we should be publicly accountable for everything." This was not just hindsight. Having seen once
again the value of setting up external mechanisms to ensure one's vir-
tue, Graham became a zealous advocate of full disclosure by parachurch organizations and in 1979 had played a key role in founding
the Evangelical Council for Financial Accountability. "If you give to
any Christian charity (including the Billy Graham Evangelistic Association)," he wrote in 1983, "and you don't insist on an understandable
financial accounting of your gift, you are in danger of falling prey to
[dishonesty]."

Despite the importance of financial probity to a ministry's reputation, most people who are aware of the Modesto Manifesto, particularly the journalists who have brought it to public attention, probably
think of it primarily because of the measures Billy Graham and his associates took to avoid illicit sexual entanglements. Students of charismatic leaders have often noted that such men tend to stir a variety of
emotions in the bosoms of their followers, a robust portion of which
feelings are distinctly sexual. Leading a movement requires enormous
energy, and the lines between political, spiritual, and sexual energy are
not finely drawn on the map of the human psyche. That dynamic
leaders, including religious leaders, experience and arouse strong sexual feeling should come as no particular surprise to anyone who pays
attention.

The journalist and biographer Marshall Frady once likened Graham to Billy Budd, a man with "exactly that quality of raw childlike
unblinking goodness," possessing "a staggering passion for the pure,

the sanitary, the wholesome, the upright." The allusion to Melville's classic *American Innocent* is a natural one, and by no means completely off the mark, but it falls short at a crucial point, and that point is a theological one. Billy Budd was naturally good and unable to believe that others did not share his elemental guilelessness. Billy Graham suffered from no such fantasies. He indeed seemed to have "a passion for the pure," but never for a minute did he imagine that he, or anyone else, was beyond corruption. And that was the secret of his ability to avoid public scandal. No one who listened to Graham warn against succumbing to the pleasures of the flesh would imagine that he derived his information solely from survey-research data. Just as he had the wisdom to put others in charge of the purse, he clearly understood that his best strategy for avoiding sexual temptation was to keep himself out of its path.

A COMMITMENT TO INTEGRITY

I suspect most of us can think of specific situations in which a strict application of the Modesto Manifesto would have helped people we know avoid a great deal of trouble, but it may not be realistic to think it is universally applicable. It is possible, however, to pledge and to pray for strength to uphold the fundamental principle at the heart of each of the manifesto's tenets: integrity. That effort will be aided by cultivation of the attitude that led Billy Graham to ask the questions that led to its formulation: humility. Circumstances change and measures suited for one era or arrangement may need to be adapted or amended to suit those changes, but men and women of integrity, humble enough to acknowledge their fallibility, will find in the Modesto Manifesto an attitude and approach that should serve them well in any situation. Integrity and humility are portable and never go out of date.

15

BEWARE THE GREAT ILLUSIONS

Norman Cousins once said in an editorial in the *Saturday Review* that there are no insoluble problems on earth. Dr. Henry Pitney Van Dusen, president emeritus of Union Theological Seminary in New York, took issue with him. "I know no one," he said, "who faces the facts and has taken accurate measure of the manifold symptoms of profound, perhaps mortal, sicknesses in American society and still clings to such illusions."

The American people have been sold a number of illusions that have no biblical foundation. I want to mention three of them. You might not agree with me, and that's your privilege. I once heard Walter Reuther, the labor leader in the 1950s and '60s, speak in Toronto just after he had called a strike of the United Auto Workers throughout Canada. He was addressing the Empire Club, and the leaders of the industry were there. What a cold reception he got! But he laid it on the line, even going so far as to name the salaries of some of the men who were sitting in front of him. I don't think a man in the room agreed with him, but when he was finished, they gave him a standing ovation—because he had the guts and the courage to tell it like it was.

THE ILLUSION OF PERMANENT EARTHLY PEACE

The first illusion I find prevalent in America today is that permanent peace is a reality apart from the intervention of God.

When Mrs. Golda Meir was prime minister of Israel, it was my privilege to see her during her trip to the United States. While I was waiting to be taken to her room, one of her aides told me that a man in New York had said to her: "Madam Prime Minister, why don't you Jews and Arabs sit down and settle your problems like Christians?" And I said: "Like in northern Ireland?"

Jesus predicted many centuries ago that we would have wars and rumors of wars to the end of time. Now why did he say that? Not because he approved of war. He said it because he knew human nature—knew its lust and its greed and its hate. Without God's help, man is not capable of solving the war problem.

Where does war come from? James the apostle tells us: "Come they not hence, even of your lusts that war in your members?" (James 4:1). In other words, we have something down inside us that is at war. As long as that spiritual war goes on in individual hearts all over the world, all other kinds of war remain possible. I read recently that there are currently at least twenty-nine wars going on in the world. Right now. This includes such conflicts as the conflict in Afghanistan, civil uprising in Libya, the Yemini al-Qaeda crackdown, and the many tribal wars in Africa. Twenty-nine wars—in a time of relative peace.

Does this mean that there is never going to be real peace? No. The Bible says there is going to be peace. The human race is not headed for destruction; we're not going to destroy ourselves. The Bible teaches that God is going to intervene in the affairs of men and that we are going to know permanent world peace. The human race is headed toward utopia. Micah the prophet said, "He shall judge among many people, and rebuke strong nations afar off; and they shall beat their swords into plowshares, and their spears into pruning hooks: nation shall not lift up a sword against nation, neither shall they learn war anymore" (Micah 4:3).

There is indeed a day of peace coming, but God is going to bring it, and it is going to be on his terms. The Jew looks for the Messiah, and the Christian looks for the Messiah also. The difference is that the Christian says that Jesus is the Messiah. But there is going to be a Messiah. There is going to be a person who can bring about peace in our world.

However, we don't have to wait till that day comes to have peace in our own hearts. "Peace I leave with you, my peace I give unto you," says Jesus (John 14:27). "I can give you a supernatural peace and security, a supernatural love and joy that you've never known, if you put your confidence and your faith and trust in me."

THE ILLUSION OF A MATERIAL UTOPIA

The second illusion that I think millions of Americans hold is that economic utopia is the answer to man's deepest needs. Advertising has sold us a bill of goods and created an expectation gap. We're told that if we use a certain kind of deodorant or a certain type of soap, we'll find happiness and peace and serenity and security. Well, suppose that all of us could have everything we wanted. Suppose there were two swimming pools in every home, three cars in every garage, a dozen chickens in every pot. Would that give us happiness and peace? No. Jesus said, "A man's life consisteth not in the abundance of the things which he possesseth" (Luke 12:15). He also said: "Man shall not live by bread alone" (Matthew 4:4). Man has much deeper needs. He needs solutions to loneliness, emptiness, alienation, guilt, the fear of death—these are his real problems.

Anna Freud, the daughter of Sigmund Freud, was asked why students riot and demonstrate. She replied: "The real reason is that fundamentally students are empty and alienated, and theirs is a burning quest for reality." I spent a lot of time at colleges and universities, and I can tell you that one of the gut issues on campus has been the search for reality: "Where did I come from? Why am I here? Where am I going?" Modern education is not answering these questions that burn in the hearts of millions of students in America and throughout the world. A friend of mine who is a film star had a son attending Berkeley back in the sixties. This boy came to his father and said, "Dad, I'm dropping out; I'm going to become a hippie." The father said, "Why?"

And the son said, "Well, Dad, I hate you." The father was of course shaken by that. "Why do you hate me?" he asked. His son said, "All right, Dad, I'll tell you. You've made it too easy for me. I've had everything and you didn't give me anything to believe in. And I hate you for it."

We've given our children the idea that material wealth is the answer—the higher the standard of living, the greater our happiness and peace. But our young people are rejecting that concept. They are lashing out and saying, "We don't want it. We're going to burn it down."

THE ILLUSION OF DEMOCRACY WITHOUT GOD

The third illusion I see prevalent in America today is the assumption that democracy can survive without a religious faith. The direction in which we are now going—toward total secularism and total materialism—will lead ultimately to suppression and dictatorship. When honesty, integrity, and morality go, democracy is in jeopardy. Marcus Aurelius once said: "When a people lose confidence in themselves, the society crumbles." We in America have become so self-critical that we are in danger of losing confidence in ourselves as a people.

Something very dangerous is happening: a vacuum is developing in philosophical America. The spirit of this new religion is antidemocratic, according to Martin Gross, writing in the *Miami Herald*, for it supposes that truth is magically revealed only to an elite following. It claims to know better than the people—a spiritual lie that imprisons man. America broke that lie when it created a republic and a democracy with its base in religion, he says. To yield now to an ancient falsehood with a fashionable new religion would be pure folly.

What we need most in America today is a revitalization of Judeo-Christianity. We must have a renewal of faith in God, faith in one another, faith in America, faith in everything our country is supposed to stand for. Without that renewal, without a revitalization of the church, the educational system, the government structure, and the mass media, our survival as a free democracy is, it seems to me, improbable.

> *Without a revitalization of the church, the educational system, the government structure, and the mass media, our survival as a free democracy is improbable.*

This renewal can begin right here in my heart and in yours, if we will rededicate our lives to the God of our fathers. Not only would such a rededication transform our personal lives and our personal relationships; it would also enable us to make the greatest contribution possible to the nation that we love and to the world in which we live.

16

WHEN TOLERANCE BECOMES SIN

One of the pet words of this age is *tolerance*. It is a good word, but we have tried to stretch it over too great an area of life. We have applied it too often where it does not belong. The word *tolerant* means "liberal," "broad-minded," "willing to put up with beliefs opposed to one's convictions," and "the allowance of something not wholly approved."

Tolerance, in one sense, implies the compromise of one's convictions, a yielding of ground upon important issues. Hence, over-tolerance in moral issues has made us soft, flabby, and devoid of conviction.

We have become tolerant about divorce; we have become tolerant about the use of alcohol; we have become tolerant about delinquency; we have become tolerant about wickedness in high places; we have become tolerant about immorality; we have become tolerant about crime; and we have become tolerant about godlessness. We have become tolerant of unbelief.

In a book published several years ago on what prominent people believe, sixty out of one hundred did not even mention God, and only eleven out of one hundred mentioned Jesus. There was a manifest tolerance toward soft character and broad-mindedness about morals, characteristic of our day. We have been sapped of conviction, drained of our beliefs, and left bereft of our faith.

THE WAY IS NARROW

The sciences, however, call for narrow-mindedness. There is no room for broad-mindedness in the laboratory. Water boils at 212 degrees Fahrenheit at sea level. It is never 100 degrees nor 189 degrees—but always 212. Water freezes at 32 degrees—not at 23 or 31.

Objects heavier than air are always attracted to the center of the earth. They always go down—never up. I know this is very narrow, but the law of gravity decrees it so, and science is narrow.

Take mathematics. The sum of two plus two is four—not three and one-half. That seems very narrow, but arithmetic is not broad. Neither is geometry. It says that a straight line is the shortest distance between two points. That seems very dogmatic and narrow, but geometry is intolerant.

A compass will always point to the magnetic north. It seems that is a very narrow view, but a compass is not very "broad-minded." If it were, all the ships at sea and all the planes in the air would be in danger.

If you should ask a man the directions to New York City and he said, "Oh, just take any road you wish; they all lead there," you would question either his sanity or his truthfulness. Somehow, we have gotten it into our minds that "all roads lead to heaven." You hear people say, "Do your best," "Be honest," and "Be sincere—and you will make it to heaven all right."

But Jesus Christ, who journeyed from heaven to earth and back to heaven again—who knew the way better than any man who ever lived—said, "Enter ye in at the strait gate: for wide is the gate, and broad is the way, that leadeth to destruction, and many there be which go in thereat: because strait is the gate, and narrow is the way, which leadeth unto life, and few there be that find it" (Matthew 7:13–14).

Jesus was narrow about the way of salvation. He plainly pointed out that there are two roads in life. One is broad—lacking in faith, convictions, and morals. It is the easy, popular, careless way. It is the way of the crowd, the way of the majority, the way of the world. He said, "Many there be that go in thereat." But he pointed out that this road, easy though it is, popular though it may be, heavily traveled though it is, leads to destruction. And in loving, compassionate intolerance he says, "Enter ye in at the strait gate . . . because strait is the gate, and narrow is the way, which leadeth unto life."

OUR LORD'S INTOLERANCE

His was the intolerance of a pilot who maneuvers his plane through the storm, realizing that a single error, just one flash of broad-mindedness, might bring disaster to all those passengers on the plane.

Once while flying from Korea to Japan, we ran through a rough snowstorm; and when we arrived over the airport in Tokyo, the ceiling and visibility were almost zero. The pilot had to make an instrument landing. I sat up in the cockpit with the pilot and watched him sweat it out as he was brought in by ground control approach. A man in the tower at the airport talked us in. I did not want these men to be broad-minded, but narrow-minded. I knew that our lives depended on it. Just so, when we come in for the landing in the great airport in heaven, I don't want any broad-mindedness. I want to come in on the beam. And even though I may be considered narrow here, I want to be sure of a safe landing there.

Christ was so intolerant of man's lost estate that he left his lofty throne in heaven, took on himself the form of man, suffered at the hands of evil men, and died on a cross to purchase our redemption. So serious was man's plight that he could not look upon it lightly. With the love that was his, he could not be broad-minded about a world held captive by its lusts, its appetites, and its sins.

Having paid such a price, Jesus could not be tolerant about man's indifference toward him and the redemption he had wrought. He said, "He that is not with me is against me" (Matthew 12:30). He also said, "He that believeth on the Son hath everlasting life: and he that believeth not the Son shall not see life; but the wrath of God abideth on him" (John 3:36).

He spoke of two roads, two kingdoms, two masters, two rewards, and two eternities. And He said, "Ye cannot serve God and mammon" (Matthew 6:24). We have the power to choose whom we will serve, but the alternative to choosing Christ brings certain destruction. Christ said that! The broad, wide, easy, popular way leads to death and destruction. Only the way of the cross leads home.

PLAYING BOTH SIDES

The popular, tolerant attitude toward the gospel of Christ is like a man going to watch the Braves and the Dodgers play a baseball game and rooting for both sides. It would be impossible for a man who has no loyalty to a particular team to really get into the game.

Baseball fans are very intolerant in both Atlanta and Los Angeles. If you would cheer for both sides in Los Angeles or Atlanta, someone would yell, "Hey, make up your mind who you're for!"

Christ said, "No man can serve two masters. . . . Ye cannot serve God and mammon" (Matthew 6:24). One of the sins of this age is the sin of broad-mindedness. We need more people who will step out and say unashamedly, "As for me and my house, we will serve the Lord" (Joshua 24:15).

Jesus Was Intolerant toward Hypocrisy

He pronounced more "woes" on the Pharisees than on any other sect because they were given to outward piety but inward sham. "Woe unto you, scribes and Pharisees, hypocrites!" he said, "for ye make clean the outside of the cup and of the platter, but within they are full of extortion and excess" (Matthew 23:25).

God has no tolerance for all talk and no action. He insists that those who profess Christ must discipline their lives to perform accordingly. The church is a stage where all the performers are professors, but where too few of the professors are performers. A counterfeit Christian can, singlehandedly, do more to retard the progress of the church than a dozen saints can do to forward it. That is why Jesus was so intolerant of sham!

> *The church is a stage where all the performers are professors, but where too few of the professors are performers.*

Sham's only reward is everlasting destruction. It is the only sin that has no reward in this life. Robbers have their loot; murderers their revenge; drunkards their stimulation; but the hypocrite has nothing but the contempt of his neighbors and the judgment of God hereafter. That is why Jesus said, "Be not, as the hypocrites" (Matthew 6:16).

Jesus Was Intolerant toward Selfishness

He said, "If any man will come after me, let him deny himself" (Luke 9:23). Self-centeredness is the basic cause of much of our distress in life. Hypochondria, a mental disorder which is accompanied by melancholy and depression, is often caused by self-pity and self-centeredness.

Most of us suffer from spiritual nearsightedness. Our interests, our loves, and our energies are too often focused upon ourselves. Jesus underscored the fact that his disciples were to live outflowingly rather than selfishly. To the rich young ruler he said, "If thou wilt be perfect, go and sell that thou hast, and give to the poor, and thou shalt have treasure in heaven" (Matthew 19:21). It wasn't the giving of the man's goods that Jesus demanded, particularly—but his release from selfishness and its devastating effect on his personality and life.

Jesus was intolerant of selfishness when he said, "For whosoever will save his life shall lose it: and whosoever will lose his life for my sake shall find it" (Matthew 16:25). The "life" that Jesus urges us to lose is the selfishness that lives within us, the old nature of sin that is in conflict with God. Peter, James, and John left their nets, but Jesus did not object to nets as such—it was the selfish living they symbolized that he wanted them to forsake. Matthew left the "custom seat," a political job, to follow Christ. But Jesus did not object to a political career as such—it was the selfish quality of living which it represented that he wanted Matthew to forsake.

So, in your life and mine, "self" must be crucified and Christ enthroned. Jesus was intolerant of any other way, for he knew that selfishness and the Spirit of God cannot exist together.

Jesus Was Intolerant toward Sin

He was tolerant toward the sinner but intolerant toward the evil that enslaved sinners. To the adulteress Jesus said, "Neither do I condemn thee: go, and sin no more" (John 8:11). He forgave her because he loved her; but he condemned sin because he loathed it with a holy hatred.

God has always been intolerant of sin! His Word says: "Wash you, make you clean; put away the evil of your doings from before mine eyes; cease to do evil" (Isaiah 1:16). "Awake to righteousness, and sin not" (1 Corinthians 15:34). "Let the wicked forsake his way, and the unrighteous man his thoughts" (Isaiah 55:7).

Christ was so intolerant of sin that he died on the cross to free men from its power. "For God so loved the world, that he gave his only begotten Son, that whosoever believeth in him should not perish, but have everlasting life" (John 3:16). Sin lies at the root of society's difficulties today. Whatever separates man from God disunites man from man. The world problem will never be solved until the question of sin is settled.

But the cross is God's answer to sin. To all who will receive the blessed news of salvation through Christ, it forever crosses out and cancels sin's power. Forest rangers know well the value of the "burn back" in fighting forest fires. To save an area from being burned, they simply burn away all of the trees and shrubs to a safe distance; and when the fire reaches that burned-out spot, those standing beyond that place are safe from the flames. Fire is thus fought by fire.

Calvary was a colossal fighting of fire by fire. Christ, taking on himself all of our sins, allowed the fire of sin's judgment to fall upon him. The area around the cross has become a place of refuge for all who would escape the judgment of sin. Take your place with him at the cross; stand by the cross; yield your life to him who redeemed you on the cross, and the fire of sin's judgment can never touch you.

God is intolerant of sin. That intolerance sent his Son to die for us. He has said "that whosoever believeth in him shall not perish." The clear implication is that those who refuse to believe in Christ shall be eternally lost. Come to him today, while his Spirit deals with your heart!

17

CONFRONTING RACISM

Racial and ethnic hostility is still one of the foremost social problems facing our world today. From the systematic horror of "ethnic cleansing" in Bosnia to the random violence ravaging our inner cities to the racial hatemongering that still permeates our society, our world seems caught up in a tidal wave of racial and ethnic tension. This hostility threatens the very foundations of modern society.

We must not underestimate the devastating effects of racism on our world. Daily headlines chronicle its grim toll: divided nations and families, devastating wars and human suffering on an unimaginable scale, a constant downward spiral of poverty and hopelessness, children cruelly broken in body and warped in heart and mind. The list is long, but for the sensitive Christian, it is even longer: whole peoples poisoned by violence and racial hatred and closed to the gospel as a result; indifference and resistance by Christians who are intolerant toward those of other backgrounds, ignoring their spiritual and physical needs.

Racism—in the world and in the church—is one of the greatest barriers to world evangelization.

Racial and ethnic hatred is a sin, and we need to label it as such. Jesus told his disciples to "love your neighbor as yourself" (Matthew 22:39 NIV); and in reply to the question "Who is my neighbor?" he responded with a pointed parable about a good Samaritan, a member of a despised race (Luke 10:25–37).

Racism is a sin precisely because it keeps us from obeying God's command to love our neighbor, and because it has its roots in pride and arrogance. Christians who harbor racism in their attitudes or actions are not following their Lord at this point, for Christ came to bring reconciliation—reconciliation between us and God, and reconciliation between each other. He came to accept us as we are, whoever we are, "from every tribe and language and people and nation" (Revelation 5:9 NIV).

Tragically, too often in the past, evangelical Christians have turned a blind eye to racism or have been willing to stand aside while others took the lead in racial reconciliation, saying it was not our responsibility. (I admit I share in that blame.) As a result, many efforts toward reconciliation in America have lacked a Christian foundation

> *Our consciences should be stirred to repentance by how far we have fallen short of what God asks us to be as his agents of reconciliation.*

and may not outlive the immediate circumstances that brought them into existence. Our consciences should be stirred to repentance by how far we have fallen short of what God asks us to be as his agents of reconciliation.

Racism, therefore, is not only a social problem: because racism is a sin, it is also a moral and spiritual issue. Legal and social efforts to obliterate racism (or at least to curb its more onerous effects) have a legitimate place. Only the supernatural love of God, however, can change our hearts in a lasting way and replace hatred and indifference with love and active compassion.

No other force exists besides the church that can bring people together week after week and deal with their deepest hurts and suspicions. Of all people, Christians should be the most active in reaching out to those of other races, instead of accepting the status quo of division and animosity.

The issues that face us are complex and enormous, and simply wishing they would go away will not solve them. I do not pretend to know the full answer. But let those of us who claim the name of Christ repent of our past failures and, relying on the Holy Spirit, demonstrate to a weary and frightened world that Christ indeed "has destroyed the barrier, the dividing wall of hostility . . . through the cross, by which he put to death their hostility" (Ephesians 2:14–16 NIV).

Part Four

MY CHALLENGE
TO GOD'S PEOPLE

18

The Hero of the Evangelicals

By Philip Yancey

As an editor at Christianity Today, *Philip Yancey covered Graham crusades. As Yancey has continued to write for* CT *and publish books like* The Jesus I Never Knew *and* What's So Amazing About Grace, *Graham said of him, "There is no writer in the evangelical world that I admire and appreciate more."*

The fundamentalist church of my youth viewed the upstart evangelist Billy Graham with deep suspicion. He invited members of the National Council of Churches—and even Roman Catholics!—to sit on his crusade platforms. He seemed soft on communism, especially in his comments about the church behind the Iron Curtain. Perhaps most important in those days of Jim Crow racism, he insisted on integrated crusades even in white bastions like Alabama.

Those suspicions, which now appear quaintly extremist, give a clue to what theologically conservative churches might have become apart from Graham's influence: cultic and divisive, a minority that defensively opposed rather than engaged culture. We can measure the greatness of the man by noting his impression on a movement that emerged from fundamentalist roots. Billy Graham did not invent the word *evangelical*, but he managed to restore the word's original meaning—*good news*—both for the skeptical world and for the beleaguered minority who looked to him for inspiration and leadership.

He made mistakes along the way, of course: angering President Truman by using the White House as a photo op, making off-the-cuff comments about social issues of the day, getting conned by President Nixon. Each time, however, he admitted his mistake and learned from it. He showed that an evangelical Christian could be both respectable and relevant, all the while clinging to a simple gospel message of God's love for sinners. As he traveled internationally, sophisticated religious leaders in places like Great Britain and Germany subjected him to scornful criticism until he met with them and disarmed them with humility and grace.

In some ways, Graham lived the quintessential American story. He rose from a modest background on a farm, working along the way as a Fuller Brush salesman, only to achieve worldwide renown. Yet one need only compare him to those featured daily on celebrity gossip shows to see a stark difference. He never cashed in financially, never partied all night or used drugs or bought mansions on Caribbean islands. Though he dined with kings, queens, premiers, and presidents, he preferred a simple life back home in North Carolina in a house jerry-built from century-old cabins.

For the millions who followed him, Graham seemed at once larger than life and yet a representative of *our* lives. He had a loyal wife who put up with his relentless travel schedule, a couple of sons who went through a rebellious period before finding themselves, two daughters who experienced the trauma of failed marriages. He struggled with health issues, occasional indecision, and management headaches. But when he stepped behind a pulpit, whether speaking to a small group at the White House or the Kremlin, or to tens of thousands gathered outdoors in Korea or in New York's Central Park, something supernatural happened. All other concerns of life faded away, and he focused like a laser beam on the one sure thing he knew: the gospel of Jesus Christ and its power to change lives.

I had the privilege of interviewing Billy Graham twice in his home, and like most journalists, I came away struck with how insecure he seemed at the core. He kept raising questions: Why hadn't his crusades had more effect on cities? Had he erred by dabbling in politics? Had the era of evangelistic crusades passed?

Meanwhile, Graham's world stature continued to grow. A record fifty-plus times he ranked among the top ten "most admired persons" in Gallup polls. A *Time* bureau chief wrote a book hailing him as one of the "great souls" of the last century, and in 2007 the magazine devoted a cover story to his relationship with eleven successive U.S. presidents. The nation had lurched through the tumultuous 1960s, survived a terrifying nuclear arms race, and entered an age of international terrorism and planetary threats. Somehow with each change, Graham and his old-fashioned message seemed even more relevant.

Graham attracted criticism for not being prophetic enough; Jesse

Jackson once mused that he would have been playing golf with the pharaohs rather than leading the slaves to liberation. Cautiously, though, he managed to tackle the great issues of the day: race, poverty, nuclear terror, communism. From the beginning of his career to the end, he truly believed that the secret to peace in the world or in any human soul traced back to the underlying issue of peace with God.

Evangelicals are a beleaguered minority no longer. We have solid programs in education, publishing, youth work, church growth, and international missions (all influenced by Graham). We have unprecedented access to power and unprecedented opportunity to shape a culture under constant threat. That is Billy Graham's legacy. He provided an important stage in maturity for those committed to planting settlements of the kingdom of God in a field full of tares. Now that he has gone, a giant question mark looms over us: can we accept his mantle and move forward in that same spirit?

19

CHOOSE LEADERS WHO
RELY ON GOD

On that tragic day when the assassination of President John F. Kennedy transferred the torch of leadership to Lyndon Johnson, I happened to be with a long-term friend of the new president. We went immediately to a quiet place to ask God to sustain him for the immense responsibilities which were thrust so suddenly upon him. That afternoon, when he was placing his hand on the Bible and being sworn in to the high office of president of the United States, we read together a passage of Holy Scripture. It was the prayer of King Solomon upon his ascension to the throne of Israel after the death of his father, King David.

A little over a year later when Johnson took that oath again and became president in his own right, I could still think of no finer prayer to begin with than that one.

In that night did God appear unto Solomon, and said unto him, Ask what I shall give thee.

And Solomon said unto God. . . . Give me now wisdom and knowledge, that I may go out and come in before this people. . . .

And God said to Solomon, Because this was in thine heart, and thou hast not asked riches, wealth, or honour, nor the life of thine enemies . . . but hast asked wisdom and knowledge for thyself, that thou mayest judge my people, over whom I have made thee king:

Wisdom and knowledge is granted unto thee; and I will give thee riches, and wealth, and honour, such as none of the kings have had that have been before thee. (2 Chronicles 1:7–12)

Just a few months after taking his first presidential oath, President Johnson said, "No man can live where I live now, nor work at the desk where I work now, without needing and without seeking the strength and support of earnest and frequent prayer." Humbled by the magnitude of the responsibilities of a high office, a man begins to probe the erratic swirl of events for a prophetic understanding of history; and when he is a spiritually sensitive man, he will feel as Lincoln did that he is a "humble instrument in the hands of Almighty God."

The National Need for Spiritual Moorings

Our national leaders today must make decisions of state perhaps greater than those of any of their predecessors. They hold in their hands the destiny not only of America but also of the world. They lead the richest and the most powerful nation the world has ever known. It is a nation that has been abundantly endowed with material blessings, but it is also a nation in danger of losing its moral moorings and its spiritual perspective. Christ, in whom are hid all the treasures of wisdom, said, "What shall it profit a man, if he shall gain the whole world, and lose his own soul?" (Mark 8:36). This applies to nations as well as to individuals, for a nation that loses its spiritual courage will grow old before its time. Even if we gain all our material and social objectives but lose our souls, it would be disastrous. As President Johnson's vice president, Hubert Humphrey, said, "It is not enough for us to have abundance; we must also have the spirit."

Both President Johnson and his vice president recognized that there is a spiritual dimension to leadership. Theodore Roosevelt once said, "The White House is a bully pulpit." So it is! From their offices in Washington, D.C., our nation's leaders have the opportunity to lead this country to new heights of social justice and economic prosperity. They also have the opportunity to lead the nation to its greatest moral and spiritual heights. Jesus Christ said, "Unto whomsoever much is given, of

Those who have the greatest power always need the greatest guidance.

him shall be much required" (Luke 12:48). Those who have the greatest power always need the greatest guidance.

No government rules except by the will of God. Our leaders occupy their offices not just as a result of the mandate of the American people, but because there is a mandate higher than the ballot box. They not only have responsibilities to all the people of America and to the peoples of the world; they also have a great responsibility to the God of our fathers.

A Solution to Our Problems?

Even to the most casual observer, it is apparent that there is a growing spiritual vacuum in our nation. Our wealth and our prosperity are in danger of making us complacent and careless in the matters of the spirit. Jesus said, "Man shall not live by bread alone" (Matthew 4:4). Many nations have tried it and failed. Germany declared neutrality in matters of religion during the thirties. That neutrality created a spiritual vacuum, and the first robust philosophy to come along filled that vacuum with a vengeance. And that, in my judgment, is how we got Nazism and the hell of World War II. The Bible plainly says, "Where there is no vision, the people perish" (Proverbs 29:18).

In foreign affairs, we are faced with overwhelming problems, from south of our own border to the Middle East to the Far East. In domestic affairs, we are faced with high unemployment, economic crises, an alarming crime rate, a moral crisis, and many individual psychological problems filling our hospitals. These problems will become more intense and more demanding in future years.

There seems to be no permanent solution to our problems. We try this scheme and that, but we find that each one is only a stopgap measure. Could it be that we have failed to properly diagnose the ills of the world? Could General MacArthur have been right when in the days of World War II he said, "The problem, basically, is theological. . . . There must be a revival of the spirit if we are to save the flesh."

I have known the leaders of several administrations well enough to know that they believe General MacArthur was right—that our problems are basically spiritual and that they require a spiritual solution. That spiritual solution was outlined by God to King Solomon long ago, when he said, "If my people, which are called by my name, shall humble themselves, and pray, and seek my face, and turn from their wicked ways; then will I hear from heaven, and will forgive their sin, and will heal their land" (2 Chronicles 7:14).

To approach the problems of the next four years in a spirit of prayer and humble dependence upon God would bring a freshness of vision and purpose that could capture the imagination of the world.

During the tenure of any administration, there are inevitable moments of discouragement, despondency, and even disillusionment. There may come times when our leaders feel as Woodrow Wilson did when the Senate voted against the ratification of his proposal for the League of Nations. When the news was telephoned to the White House, Wilson said, "I feel like going to bed and staying there." He could not sleep that night, and he turned to his personal physician and close friend, Dr. Cary T. Grayson, at about three o'clock in the morning and said, "Doctor, the devil is a busy man."

Later in the morning, he had Grayson read St. Paul's consoling words from 2 Corinthians: "We are troubled on every side, yet not distressed; we are perplexed . . . but not forsaken; cast down, but not destroyed" (4:8–9). Turning to Grayson, President Wilson said, "Doctor, if I were not a Christian, I think I should go mad, but my faith in God holds me to the belief that he is, in some way, working out his own plans, in spite of human mistakes."

Centuries ago Moses stood before the people of Israel and said, "When thou art in tribulation, and all these things are come upon thee . . . if thou turn to the Lord thy God, and shalt be obedient unto his voice; . . . he will not forsake thee, . . . nor forget the covenant of thy fathers which he sware unto them" (Deuteronomy 4:30–31).

In the midst of the Civil War, Abraham Lincoln read his Bible regularly. He memorized passages from its pages. He used the Word of God to help him make decisions and solve problems. In matters of right and wrong, the God of the Bible was Lincoln's final court of appeals. The overwhelming problems of his day drove him to the Scriptures and to his knees in prayer. Out of this humble dependence on God came the preservation of the Union.

History throbs with crises, but the gospel is that God is *for* man, and that, in the greatest crisis this world has ever known—when Jesus Christ went to the cross—God transformed that tragedy into triumph and wrought redemption for those who trust in him.

The Need for Leaders with Personal Faith

On the wall of President Johnson's office at the White House, I remember seeing a framed, yellowed letter. It was written to Johnson's great-grandfather Baines more than one hundred years earlier, and it bore the bold—almost defiant—signature of Sam Houston.

The reason for the letter was that President Johnson's great-grandfather led General Sam Houston to a saving knowledge of Jesus Christ. This conversion transformed that troubled, rough hero of San Jacinto into a man of peace, happiness, and purpose. As Marquis James put it in his biography of Houston, *The Raven*:

> The long quest for spiritual repose ended when Houston knelt before the altar and asked to be received into the Church, and on the 19th of November, 1858, the convert waded into the chilly waters of Rocky Creek, and was baptized. A church publication at that time said, "The announcement of General Houston's conversion has excited wonder and surprise of many who have supposed that he was past praying for."[1]

At the time, somebody said to Sam Houston, "Well, General, I hear all your sins were washed away." "I hope so," Sam Houston replied, "but if they were all washed away, the Lord help the fish down below."

On the day Sam Houston was baptized, he offered to pay half the minister's salary in the church. When someone asked him about it, he said, "My pocketbook was baptized, too."

This newness of spiritual life that the president's great-grandfather Baines helped introduce to General Sam Houston is the same transforming faith we need in our nation today if we are to successfully meet our rendezvous with destiny. That letter, written by a heroic Texan to the great-grandfather of one of our presidents, is heartening evidence of a sense of moral direction. The letter itself is important, but the fact that the president chose to hang it in his office is also important. It is a shining symbol that from the very apex of government, there was a desire for a spiritual emphasis in our national affairs.

Our nation was founded on spiritual principles. In our Declaration of Independence, our founding fathers recognized a dependence on God and our need for him. And by far the majority of them were men who recognized the nation's continuing need for leaders who acknowledged an active dependence on God. That is why I found it so encouraging that our thirty-sixth president—and others since—openly expressed reliance on God. The letter from Sam Houston that Lyndon Baines Johnson hung in his office said symbolically that he had respect for the "old faith" that had guided his family, his state, and his nation through generations.

As this great nation goes forward under its continuing succession of leaders, I pray that we the people of the United States will take care to elect leaders who exhibit such a faith. I pray that each administration will rededicate itself to those moral and spiritual principles that have undergirded the nation from its beginning.

20

RECOVER THE PRIORITY OF EVANGELISM

We stand only years into the third millennium after the birth of our Savior. Never has the Christian church faced so many challenges on so many fronts—political, social, demographic, economic, and philosophical.

In response to these challenges, the church today often seems paralyzed and confused, torn by division and uncertainty. Instead of being salt and light in the world, we have been content to withdraw into our separate ecclesiastical ghettos, preoccupied with our own internal affairs and unconcerned about the deepest needs of those around us. In the eyes of many, religion has lost its relevance and is little more than a quaint relic from another time.

In spite of the difficulties, the twenty-first century could mark the greatest evangelistic advance in the history of the Christian church. In order for this to happen, however, the church (in all of its diversity) must embrace the challenges it faces and must mobilize every possible spiritual and physical resource to declare the gospel that has been committed to us.

THE CHALLENGES WE NOW FACE

I see at least four trends in particular that now pose a special challenge to Christian evangelism.

Uncontrolled Urbanization

The world's population now hovers at a staggering seven billion people—approximately three times the number of people living at the dawn of the twentieth century. At least half of those people are living in large cities—uprooted from their past, transient, often struggling for survival in the midst of extreme poverty, and potentially explosive politically because their dreams may have ended in disillusionment and despair. Over 50 percent of the world's population is under twenty-five years of age, and in the poorer parts of the world that number is much higher.

Unrelenting Aggressive Secularism

One of the most discouraging historical trends over the past century or more has been the "de-Christianization" of many former Christian strongholds (particularly in Europe) because of the massive onslaught of secularism. Secularism, however, has an increasing impact in other parts of the world, such as Southeast Asia. Most people who lived in the former communist nations of Eastern Europe did not abandon their secular outlook, even though they may have jettisoned its Marxist trappings.

Secularism can take many attitudes toward religion, from total indifference to virulent hostility. At its root, however, secularism always excludes God from the world and from daily human life, and the secularist lives for the present without any reference to God or divine moral and spiritual absolutes. People with a secular outlook on life often feel very little need of religion, and therefore are indifferent or not open to the Christian message.

Expanding Non-Christian Religions

While secularism is growing in some parts of the world, other parts are experiencing a profound religious reawakening. One reason is a growing suspicion that secularism has failed to provide real answers to life's ultimate questions. As a result, some non-Christian religions have grown increasingly suspicious of Western secular trends, believing they could sound the death knell of their religious traditions. In many instances, as in the case of Islam, they have grown increasingly militant and aggressive, and some nations that have officially adopted one of these as their sole religion have passed new laws restricting Christian influence and activity.

Even in countries like the United States, there has been an upsurge in religious interest. Not all of this religious interest, however, has been focused on historic Christianity; cults and non-Western religious traditions have also experienced growth.

Shifting Frontiers and Emerging Fields

The last decade of the twentieth century will be remembered by historians as one of the watershed periods of the modern era. The collapse of Marxism in Eastern Europe and the old Soviet Union brought about staggering changes, the full impact of which we cannot fully assess even yet.

From the standpoint of Christian evangelism, however, it marked one of the greatest openings for the gospel in the history of the church. Never before has such a vast area, encompassing hundreds of millions of people, opened so suddenly and thoroughly to evangelistic activity. In most of these areas a remnant of the church survived the fierce onslaughts of atheism, but the task of evangelizing their lands cannot be done by these churches alone. Those who evangelize from outside, however, must learn to temper their enthusiasm with prayer, strategic thinking, cultural sensitivity, and a willingness to work as partners with those who are already there.

What other new fields will emerge in coming decades? Will changes in the Middle East or Asia mean the door will open to Christian evangelism from other parts of the world?

As we get deeper into the twenty-first century, we may also see the closing of doors to evangelization and increasing religious polarization in some parts of the world. Some nations that have historically been Christian have already abandoned their Christian roots almost completely. They are rapidly becoming the targets of aggressive proselytizing by non-Christian religions.

THINGS THAT DO NOT CHANGE

In the midst of so many changes in the world, it is the unique function of the church to declare by word and deed that there are some things that never change. It is the message that God—the supreme, unchanging, omnipotent Creator of the universe—loves humanity and wants us to know him in a personal way. It is the message that humankind has strayed from God—rebelled against his revealed will, and as a result of sin is alienated from God and from others. It is the message that God has taken the initiative to bridge the gap between himself and sinful humanity, and he did this by coming to earth in the person of Jesus Christ. It is the message that there is hope for the future because Christ rose from the dead and will reign victorious over all the forces of evil and death and hell.

No, God has not changed, nor has the nature of the human heart changed. And that is why the gospel is relevant to every individual in every culture: beneath all the cultural, ethnic, social, economic, and political differences that separate us, the deepest needs and hurts and fears of the human heart are still the same. The gospel is still "the power of God for the salvation of everyone who believes" (Romans 1:16 NIV1984).

There is one other thing that has not changed, and that is the commission of Christ to the church to "Go into all the world and preach the good news to all creation" (Mark 16:15 NIV1984).

That command—thoroughly undergirded by a deep love for Christ and for others—impelled the early Christians to go from one end of the Roman Empire to the other, often paying the price for their commitment with their lives. In obedience to that same command, a host of missionaries and evangelists across the centuries have brought the message of God's love in Christ to the farthest corners of human civilization.

EFFECTIVE EVANGELISM IN OUR CENTURY

Will the church of Jesus Christ meet the challenge of this twenty-first century, with all its complexity and even confusion? Or will Christians retreat slowly but inexorably into steadily shrinking ecclesiastical ghettos, their message unheeded and their efforts feeble and ineffective? Now is the time for the church to honestly come to grips with those questions.

What will it take for the evangelistic imperative to be lived out in the future so that the twenty-first century becomes the greatest century for Christian evangelism in history? Let me suggest four keys to effective evangelism—basic principles in evangelism that have always been valid, but that take on special urgency given the challenges of the modern world.

A Rediscovery of the Full Biblical Message

Polls repeatedly demonstrate that if people in the Western world are asked if they believe in God, Jesus, heaven, or in other basic doctrines of the Christian faith, large numbers answer yes. And yet there is little or no evidence of vital, living faith in their lives. Why? One reason is that those same people, when asked, "What is a Christian?" have little or no comprehension of what the Bible says about that urgent question.

The evangelistic task, first of all, should send us back to our Bibles, carefully and prayerfully studying to uncover the heart of God's message to an unbelieving world. It also will mean a recovery of the biblical priority of evangelism. Sad to say, evangelism in many churches today (and for many individual Christians) seems almost an afterthought to the normal workings of the congregation or denomination.

Even a casual inspection of the New Testament will reveal that evangelism was the priority of the early church. Christians are called by God to do many things, but a church that has lost sight of the priority of evangelism has lost sight of its primary calling under God.

Biblical evangelism needs to be given much greater priority in theological education as well—in fact, it should permeate every aspect of a seminary's curriculum instead of being a minor appendage, as is too often the case.

The recovery of the priority of evangelism should not lead us, however, to make a false distinction between the proclamation of the gospel and social concern. Both are part of God's calling and must go hand in hand. A Christian who fails to express Christ's love for humanity through compassionate service is not living a life of full discipleship. In like manner, a Christian who fails to express Christ's love for humanity through clear verbal witness is also not living a life of full discipleship. Jesus, we read, "went through all the towns and villages, teaching in their synagogues, preaching the good news of the kingdom and healing every disease and sickness" (Matthew 9:35 NIV1984). Immediately afterward he commissioned the twelve disciples to go out and do likewise.

Christians today who have a special interest in evangelism have discovered in new ways the truth of this diversity of ministry. Article 5 of the Lausanne Covenant of 1974 states, "We affirm that God is both the Creator and the Judge of all. . . . We therefore should share his concern for justice and reconciliation throughout human society and for the liberation of [everyone] from every kind of oppression. . . . The salvation we claim should be transforming us in the totality of our personal and social responsibilities."

The Mobilization of the Whole Church

For too long we have assumed that evangelism was the province of only a few professionals, or a task that the pastor alone could do (in addition to the multitude of other duties the pastor faces every day). Such a view is not faithful to the New Testament, neither is it realistic if the challenges of the coming decades are to be met. The task is simply too overwhelming. Professor Michael Green has rightly said that "whenever Christianity has been at its most healthy, evangelism has stemmed from the local church and has had a noticeable impact on the surrounding area. I do not believe that the re-Christianization of the West can take place without the renewal of local churches in this whole area of evangelism."[1]

The early church spread not only by the preaching of those few who were gifted as preachers and evangelists, important as they were, but also through the quiet and faithful witness of ordinary Christians to their pagan neighbors. Paul wrote to the young Thessalonian church, "The Lord's message rang out from you not only in Macedonia and Achaia—your faith in God has become known everywhere" (1 Thessalonians 1:8 NIV1984).

The mobilization of the whole church for evangelism—including both the clergy and the laity—must be repeated today if the church is to spread the gospel effectively. Professor George Hunter has written, "Western Christianity needs a multitude of intentional missionary congregations—churches that will abandon the Christendom model of ministry as merely nurturing the faithful—whose primary mission will be to reach and disciple people who do not yet believe."[2]

This means we must focus more intently on discipleship training—training that includes evangelism. It means we repent of our compromises and our failure to demonstrate the transforming power and love of Christ in our lives, and we learn afresh what it means to be salt and light in a decaying and dark world. Often the unbelieving world rejects our message because it sees no difference between Christians and non-Christians.

> *Often the unbelieving world rejects our message because it sees no difference between Christians and non-Christians.*

It means also that we encourage the discovery and development of the spiritual gift of evangelism in all of its manifestations. Within the church, God "gave some to be apostles, some to be prophets, some to be evangelists, and some to be pastors and teachers" (Ephesians 4:11 NIV1984). That gift has never been withdrawn from the church. Some will exercise that gift with children or youth; some will exercise it with their neighbors or business associates; still others will exercise it in a public preaching ministry. However it is exercised, the special gift of evangelism should be an inherent part of the church's total ministry, not an isolated or independent work divorced from the church or even opposed by it.

Willingness to Explore New Methods and New Fields

Methods that have worked in the past to make people aware of the church and draw them into its programs will not necessarily work in a media-saturated age. It is no coincidence that those churches that are most effective in reaching their neighborhoods and cities for Christ are often those that are the most flexible and adaptable in their methods. For example, just because we think unchurched people *ought* to come to Sunday morning worship does not mean they *will* come. And if that is a church's only channel for contact with those who are not its members, it should not be surprised to see its role dwindle and few people come to faith in Christ.

In America, some churches offer Saturday evening services (in addition to those on Sunday) because they have found that unbelievers in their areas are more open to attending then. This, of course, is not necessarily the right pattern for other churches; the main point is that we need to first stand back and observe, and then be creative.

In some communities, that will mean developing specific programs to meet the needs of specialized groups—mothers, singles, single parents, teenagers, the elderly, businesspeople, and so on. Each of these groups has particular felt needs, and their felt needs often can form the point of contact between them and the church.

I do not want to be misunderstood, however. Evangelism is more than methods, and in fact, methods can get in the way of authentic evangelism. Methods are necessary, but methods also can easily become ends in themselves instead of tools or means of evangelism.

Total and Unconditional Dependence on God

To me, there has always been a wondrous mystery to the preaching of the gospel. We are commanded to be faithful in proclaiming the Word—and yet, at the same time, every success, every advance, no matter how slight, is possible only because God has been at work by the Holy Spirit. The Spirit gives us the message, leads us to those he has prepared, and brings conviction of sin and new life.

When we understand that truth, it frees us from the temptation to use manipulation or pressure. It also should free us from pride and boasting, because we know that God alone must receive the credit for whatever is accomplished.

When we understand that truth, we also will realize the urgency of prayer in evangelism. My own ministry, I am convinced, has only been possible because of the countless men and women who have prayed. I never stand before an audience without sensing those prayers and sensing also my own dependence on God the Holy Spirit to accomplish his work. The words from Zechariah should be written indelibly on our hearts and minds: "'Not by might nor by power, but by my Spirit,' says the Lord Almighty" (Zechariah 4:6 NIV).

GOD'S WORD FOR THE THIRD MILLENNIUM

As we stand inside the twenty-first century, what is God saying to us? If we are among those who have been indifferent to God, his message is clear: Come to me while there is still time. I made you; I love you; I have provided the way for you to come to know me personally by faith in Christ.

To his people, however, God is telling us to be faithful to Christ, to be faithful to his calling, to point others to Christ by our words and by our deeds. Will the twenty-first century mark the greatest advance the Christian church has ever known—or the greatest defeat?

Archbishop George Carey's words from his enthronement in April 1991 bear repeating: "It will be woe to us if we preach religion instead of the gospel. . . . Woe to us if we preach a message that looks only towards inner piety and does not relate our faith to the world around. . . . And woe to us if we fail to hand on to future generations the unsearchable riches of Christ which are the very heartbeat of the church and its mission."

That is our challenge today.

21

RESPOND TO THE HARVEST

I believe that the Holy Spirit is breaking into our nations and organizations in a new way around the world. For almost the first time in history, converts from non-Christian religions are beginning to be counted in the hundreds rather than one by one.

We must capitalize on the spirit of unrest and change throughout the world. Old political orders are tottering. Revolution and change are everywhere. The nations of the world are arming as never before. Many world leaders will admit in private that they believe the world stands on the very edge of Armageddon. But radical change and crisis are our challenge to seek creative means of evangelism. We may be living in "the last days."

I believe that we must mobilize the young people of every continent who have recently been won to Christ. I don't believe there have ever been as many committed young people worldwide as there are today. They are waiting to be challenged and led in the most decisive and the most thrilling crusade and revolution in history—*to evangelize the world!*

Churches outside America and Europe are wonderfully awakening to their responsibility in world missions. We learned just a few years ago that there are more than two hundred mission boards in churches in Africa, Asia, and Latin America. These societies channel missionaries from Korea and Indonesia and Africa into countries where we Westerners cannot go. It is our challenge as Westerners to seek new patterns of partnership whereby Christians from affluent nations can cooperate with these missionary societies in prayer, support, and fellowship.

I believe we must view nationalism not as a threat but as an opportunity. Jesus Christ was not a Westerner. We do not know what the color of his skin was. It was likely brown and swarthy, similar to the skin color prevalent in that area. He came from the world that touched Asia, Africa, and Europe—but he was God's Son, who was sent to redeem "the whole world." We must seek means to help persons in developing nations find their authentic identity in Jesus Christ, not in pagan practices.

Much of the Catholic world is a new challenge to evangelicals in our day. I spoke to ministers in Belgium several years ago and heard from them of great changes of attitude among Catholics. During a crusade in Brazil we could hardly believe our ears and eyes as we saw the sweeping changes that have taken place there, even in recent months. A missionary for almost thirty years in Colombia, South America, was preaching some time ago when a nun came to him and asked what she should do now that she had come to Christ. He replied that she should report her experience to her mother superior. She quietly answered, "I am the mother superior."

We must pray for and be prepared for evangelism in parts of the world whose doors are seemingly closed; some are already slightly ajar, and others may soon open. We must reach out to these brethren in prayer and loving fellowship wherever possible. At the same time let us believe that God is going to open a door so we can work with him in evangelism behind the various political and religious curtains.

MAINTAINING THE ESSENTIALS OF FAITH

It is always interesting to me that the most scathing denunciation that Jesus made of any group was against the Pharisees, as recorded in Matthew 23. The Pharisees had started out as a God-honoring reform movement. Judaism was in disobedience. The Jewish people refused to repent, and judgment, defeat, and exile fell upon them. Sects and parties like the Zealots, Sadducees, and Pharisees sprang up as "correctives" of the religious degeneracy that had prevailed. They sprang from a fervent passion to obey Scripture and carry out its teachings to the letter. Yet the movements all too soon succumbed to peripheral matters and other influences—until they themselves needed correcting!

Time after time in history one could point to corrective measures and movements that have arisen in the church and have eventually followed the way of the Pharisees. For example, Protestantism became a giant corrective in the sixteenth century. But in the course of time, parts of it degenerated to a lifeless formalism, nearly as bad as that against which it revolted. Kierkegaard wrote:

> Lutheranism is a "corrective," but a corrective which has been made into a norm becomes confusing to the second generation. And with each generation that adopts it, things get worse and worse, until it is seen that "the corrective" produces precisely the opposite of its original description.[1]

As Kierkegaard saw it, then, the central trouble with Lutheranism in nineteenth-century Denmark was this: a magnified belief and minimized practice.

On the other hand, during the past seventy-five years, theological liberalism and radicalism became not just innocent modifications of Christianity but in some instances a totally new and different religion—a religion that denied biblical supernaturalism, a religion that had no need for revealed truth and redemptive grace. God raised up evangelicalism not just as a corrective to this corrosive liberalism but as a vigorous reaffirmation of historic first-century Christianity.

Theological orthodoxy is absolutely essential, but it is no safeguard against spiritual degeneracy.

I believe that through many movements within the church throughout the world and through many parachurch organizations, God has once again raised up a strong evangelical leadership. I pray that we will not fall into the same trap into which our fathers fell. Theological orthodoxy is absolutely essential, but it is no safeguard against spiritual degeneracy.

MEETING THE GREATEST NEED

We have a mandate from God himself. A person's last will and command are usually considered his most important; our Lord's last command and instructions were, "Go ye into all the world, and preach the gospel to every creature" (Mark 16:15). He also said, "But ye shall receive power, after that the Holy Ghost is come upon you: and ye shall be witnesses unto me both in Jerusalem, and in all Judaea, and in Samaria, and unto the uttermost part of the earth" (Acts 1:8).

In a strange and wonderful way—the reasons known only to God—our Lord tied in his second coming with these commands when he said, "And this gospel of the kingdom shall be preached in all the world for a witness unto all nations; and then shall the end come" (Matthew 24:14).

The paramount need of the world today is for reconciliation with God, and nothing will benefit men here and now more than for them to become convinced followers and obedient disciples of the Lord Jesus Christ. We need more effective propagation of the gospel, more speedy and sound discipling of the nations.

No Compromise

In conclusion, let me plead that we not compromise the Bible as the authoritative, infallible Word of God.

The stark reality is that the battle is joined—the enemy is destructively at work. It is God versus Satan; heaven versus hell; truth versus error; the Word of God versus the word of men. But because of the victory Jesus Christ has already achieved, we know the outcome—the King of kings will establish his triumphant reign.

Early in the 1940s, several of America's leading scientists went to President Roosevelt and told him they had a formula that would end the war and change the world. On paper it was simply a few letters: "$E=mc^2$." The mathematical genius of Albert Einstein had conceived it, America's leading scientists had checked it, and from this simple formula came the secret of atomic power.

Amid all the visions, strategies, methods, plans, and programs that dedicated evangelicals have come up with, the great secret of success will be a simple formula that must control all of the thinking and planning we do as we set out to fulfill the Lord's commission. It is $E=mp^2$ (evangelism=men times prayer to the highest power).

World evangelization will be "'not by might nor by power, but by my Spirit,' says the Lord" (Zechariah 4:6 NIV). Our planning will be of no avail unless we begin, continue, and end in prayer. We must arouse Christians around the world to great waves of prayer upon whose crest evangelistic movements may flow into every nation.

Faced with Christ's life, teachings, and commands to evangelize, his disciples pleaded, "Lord, teach us to pray!" and "Lord, increase our faith." Let these be our requests as we kneel before the Lord to hasten world evangelization and the coming of the Lord in this century.

22

A BRIGHT TOMORROW

Whathat does the future hold for evangelicals? Where will evangelicalism be in another fifty years? Only God knows the future, and we can be thankful that God is the God of the future. Try as we might, our speculations about the future will be only that—speculations. If we went back a hundred years, we would be amazed at how far off target many predictions were concerning the twentieth century. History is full of surprises, and this century will be no exception. Many leaders openly question whether or not there will be another full century.

Population growth will bring new pressures and new ethical problems. Technological advances will probably be staggering, providing new opportunities for the furtherance of the gospel—and new dangers as well. Progress always has its dark side, for the human heart has not changed.

But technology alone will not determine the future of evangelicalism, nor will any other outside influence—social, political, economic, or intellectual. Yes, these will all affect us, but whether or not evangelicals once again become an insignificant minority will depend on one thing: whether we allow God to shape our hearts and minds and to guide us as we respond to a changing world. Let me mention six factors that I believe will determine the future impact of evangelicals.

First, the evangelical future will depend on *our vision*. The twin enemies of vision are always complacency and discouragement. Complacency makes us lazy; discouragement paralyzes us. Few things cripple us like pride and self-satisfaction in the face of success or despair in the face of evil. We evangelicals are no longer an ignored minority, but success should drive us to our knees, for its dangers are enormous.

How can we be complacent when over two-thirds of the world's population are not Christian, even in a nominal sense? Or how can we be discouraged when God is still at work and has promised to be with us to the end of the age?

I often think of the words of James at the Jerusalem Council, that God was at work among the nations "to take out of them a people for his name" (Acts 15:14). This is still happening all over the world. Often these new believers are a very small minority, and yet they are still a part of God's great plan.

Second, the future of evangelicalism will depend on *our trust*. There is much to lament today, and at times Satan seems to be thrashing about in one final, desperate attempt to capture this world. We must not be ignorant of his devices.

But will we fight the spiritual battles of the future in the energy of the flesh? Or will we yield ourselves to the power of the Holy Spirit, using the spiritual weapons God has provided to combat the forces of evil arrayed against us?

During our evangelistic crusade in Minneapolis in the 1990s, we witnessed one of the largest responses to the gospel message we had ever seen. I am convinced the main reason was prayer, as believers from almost every denomination (including Roman Catholics) sought the face of God in intercession for their area. These Christians sensed their own powerlessness, knowing that only God could break through the hardness of the human heart and turn back the forces of deception and darkness.

Third, the evangelical future will depend on *our obedience*. Few things discredit the gospel in the eyes of the world more quickly than moral and ethical failure by those claiming to follow Christ. And yet we are in grave danger of being captured by the spirit of our age. Satan apparently does not need to invent any new temptations; the allures of money, pleasure, and power seem quite sufficient to blunt our witness and neutralize our impact. In an ego-driven world given over to selfish indulgence and pride, Christians must be models of integrity and morality, both in their personal lives and in the work of their institutions and organizations.

Fourth, it will depend on *our love and compassion*. Just as moral compromise blunts our message, so does an unloving or indifferent spirit. Divine love sent Christ into the world, and that same love must compel us to reach out to a hurting and torn world. If we are filled with God's love, we will seek to overcome the racial and economic barriers that divide us and condemn untold millions to hopelessness and poverty. We will reach out with the gospel to those who are lost, for there is no greater way we can express love than to tell others about the Savior's love.

We also must learn in a deeper way what it means to love within the body of Christ, even when there is not full agreement. Satan surely must rejoice when there is bickering and strife among fellow believers. Overcoming disunity may well be one of our greatest challenges in the years ahead.

Fifth, the future of evangelicalism will depend on *our faithfulness to the Word of God*. One of the hallmarks of evangelicals has always been our commitment to the Bible as the unique and authoritative Word of God. Will we lose confidence in its trustworthiness, intentionally or unintentionally looking elsewhere for spiritual foundations?

There probably has never been a time in church history when the gospel was not under attack from some quarter. Those attacks have usually been most devastating, however, when they came from within. Will that be true among evangelicals in the future? Certain theological truths are not negotiable, and more than ever we must seek to be faithful to the Word of God, allowing it to shape our thinking and mold our behavior.

Finally, the future impact of evangelicals will depend on *our steadfastness*. Most of us know very little of Paul's experience: "When we are cursed, we bless; when we are persecuted, we endure it; when we are slandered, we answer kindly. Up to this moment we have become the scum of the earth, the refuse of the world" (1 Corinthians 4:12–13 NIV).

The time may come when society will turn against us; can those of us who follow the One who was despised and rejected expect anything less for ourselves? Or, in God's providence, the opposite may be the case; the massive tides of secularism sweeping our land might be reversed.

Either way, it does not matter. We are called to be steadfast for Christ and his truth, regardless of the situation. Our calling is not to be successful (as the world measures success); our calling is to be faithful.

> *Our calling is not to be successful (as the world measures success); our calling is to be faithful.*

Paul exhorted the Corinthian Christians not to give in to the pressures of their pagan culture but to hold fast to the risen Christ. His words apply just as pointedly to us today: "Stand firm. Let nothing move you. Always give yourselves fully to the work of the Lord, because you know that your labor in the Lord is not in vain" (1 Corinthians 15:58 NIV).

May we each recommit our lives to Christ and his will as we face the future.

Part Five

UPON FURTHER REFLECTION

23

Why I Founded
Christianity Today

In the late forties and early fifties, I had been deeply concerned about the situation of evangelicals in the United States. We seemed to be confused, bewildered, divided, and almost defeated in the face of the greatest opportunity and responsibility possibly in the history of the church. This burden and concern had been growing month by month. I had found that this same burden existed among many evangelical leaders.

In a sense we were almost leaderless. Many evangelical leaders had urged me from time to time to call a conference. We had begun to realize that there had been a tremendous shift in theological thinking in the church within the past ten years. We were also aware that there had been a great shift in opinion throughout America concerning

God, the Bible, the church, and the need for spiritual awakening. We had seen great segments of the church shifting back toward the orthodox and evangelical positions, while at the same time religion had grown popular in every stratum of society.

In my contacts with hundreds of clergymen throughout the United States, I found a longing and hungering on the part of many for genuine revival. There was a new emphasis on evangelism everywhere. Thousands of young ministers were really in the evangelical camp in their theological thinking and evangelistic zeal. Strange to say, however, some of our major denominations, church councils, and other organizations were directed by extreme liberals who actually did not represent the vast majority of ministers in this country.

Why? I was convinced that evangelicals were in the majority among both clergy and church members. However, we had no rallying point; we had no flag or organization under which we could all gather. We were divided, confused, and in one sense, defeated. We needed a new, strong, and vigorous voice to call us together—one that would have the respect of all evangelicals of all stripes within our major denominations.

The Need for an Evangelical Magazine

It came to me with ever-increasing conviction that one of the great needs was a religious magazine on the order of the *Christian Century*—one that would reach the clergy and the lay leaders of every denomination, presenting truth from the evangelical viewpoint. This vacuum in the United States and Britain needed to be filled.

For a long time the *Christian Century* had been and still is the voice of theological liberalism in this country. Its influence is tremendous. It is constantly quoted in *Time, Newsweek,* and other secular magazines and newspapers. Its intellectual popular journalism is a must for thousands of ministers each week. In the early fifties and earlier, it influenced religious thought more than any single factor in Protestantism, in my opinion. At that time there was no evangelical paper that had respect that could challenge it.

Therefore, I called a group of leading evangelicals and trusted friends together for prayer, consultation, and advice; to seek the will of God in this matter; and to present some concrete proposals for our discussion, prayers, and thought. I proposed to them that we found an evangelical magazine that would consist of:

1. Hard-hitting editorials on current subjects—from the evangelical viewpoint.

2. Full news coverage—that we carry all that comes over the wires of the Religious News Service, and that we have at least one hundred reporters throughout the entire world carrying all the religious news possible.

3. At least one biblical exposition in each issue by some of our greatest Bible expositors written on the highest intellectual plane, yet with a simplicity that all can understand.

4. At least one evangelistic sermon.

5. A digest of what other magazines all over the world are saying so that ministers can understand what other parts of the world are thinking religiously and theologically.

6. One section of seed thoughts and helps for pastors in their preparation of sermons.

7. Occasional good biography of the great saints of the past as inspiration and challenge to young ministers today.

8. Hard-hitting articles on subjects relating to Christianity, such as archaeology, etc.

9. Book reviews—covering not only the religious, but also many outstanding secular books.

I recommended that the editorial policy of the magazine be along the following lines:

1. Prochurch—this magazine should not take sides in fights among various councils in the United States. We should be constructive, positive, and not antichurch. I was convinced that there were thousands of ministers who could be won to evangelicalism, but they would not be driven, and the magazine's first vicious attack against some denomination or council would cause these young ministers to throw our magazine in the wastebasket. We wanted to gradually win their confidence, and then in a

thousand subtle ways point out the various weaknesses of some of our organized religion in this country. This magazine should take the responsibility of leading in love—what so much of our evangelical work has failed to do in fighting and name-calling.

2. This magazine should be thoroughly biblical, evangelical, and evangelistic. I suggested, however, that we not use the term *fundamentalist* or even *conservative*. I thought the word *evangelical* was far better and far more disarming.

3. This magazine should be nondispensational. There were thousands of ministers in this country who would support us if we took this position but would not support us if we became dispensational.

4. The magazine should be neither amillennial nor premillennial, but it certainly should be extremely pro–Second Advent. We should present the second coming of Christ in all of its glory without getting too deeply into the differing beliefs concerning the millennium.

5. This magazine must be for social improvement and address the great social issues of our day, such as the starving people around the globe, the racial problem, and others. We must be for the underdog and the downtrodden—as we all believe Christ was—without being socialistic in our tendencies.

6. This magazine should take a mildly conservative political position in our interpretation of current events (in other words, the editorial policy should be "down the middle of the road"). I believed thousands of clergymen would follow a flag planted in the center, and then they could be led quietly to a genuine orthodox position and a vigorous evangelism.

I suggested that the name of the magazine be *Christianity Today*. This was the name of a Presbyterian journal that had been discontinued some years prior. I suggested the magazine have a maximum of thirty to fifty pages; that it would be printed on the same type of paper as the *Christian Century*; that its journalism be intellectual yet popular; and that the articles be brief (we were already living in a day when even ministers would not read long, involved articles).

THE MAGAZINE SETS ITS COURSE

The response of the group was enthusiastic, and the decision was made to launch the magazine, which has since become the most widely read monthly publication among Christian leaders. *Christianity Today* had its origin in a deeply felt desire to express historical Christianity to the present generation. Neglected, slighted, misrepresented—evangelical Christianity needed a clear voice to speak with conviction and love, and to state its true position and its relevance to the world crises.

A generation has grown up unaware of the basic truths of the Christian faith taught in the Scriptures and expressed in the creeds of the historically evangelical churches.

Theological liberalism has failed to meet the moral and spiritual needs of the people. Neither the man on the street nor the intellectual is today much attracted by its preaching and

> *Theological liberalism has failed to meet the moral and spiritual needs of the people.*

theology. All too frequently, it finds itself adrift in speculation that neither solves the problem of the individual nor of the society of which he is a part.

For the preacher, an unending source of wisdom and power lies in a return to truly biblical preaching. For the layman, this same Book will prove to be light on the pathway of life, the record of the One who alone meets our needs for now and for eternity.

Christianity Today remains confident to this day that the answer to the theological confusion existing in the world is found in Christ and the Scriptures. There is evidence that more and more people are rediscovering the Word of God as their source of authority and power. Many of these searchers for the truth are unaware of the existence of an increasing group of evangelical scholars throughout the world. Through the pages of *Christianity Today*, Christian writers and leaders expound and defend the basic truths of the Christian faith in terms of reverent scholarship and of practical application to the needs of the present generation.

Those who direct the editorial policy of *Christianity Today* unreservedly accept the complete reliability and authority of the written Word of God. It is their conviction that the Scriptures teach the doctrine of plenary inspiration. This doctrine has been misrepresented and misunderstood. To state the biblical concept of inspiration is one of the aims of the magazine.

The content of historic Christianity is continually presented and defended. Among the distinctive doctrines the magazine stresses are those of God, Christ, man, salvation, and the last things. The best modern scholarship recognizes the bearing of doctrine on moral and spiritual life. This emphasis finds encouragement in the pages of *Christianity Today*.

True ecumenicity is fostered by setting forth the New Testament teaching of the unity of believers in Jesus Christ. External organic unity is not likely to succeed unless the unity engendered by the Holy Spirit prevails. A unity that endures must have as its spiritual basis a like faith, an authentic hope, and the renewing power of Christian love.

National stability and survival depend upon enduring spiritual and moral qualities. Revival as the answer to national problems may seem to be an oversimplified solution to a distressingly complex situation. Nevertheless statesmen as well as theologians realize that the basic solution to the world crisis is theological. *Christianity Today* stresses and encourages the impact of evangelism on life.

Christianity Today applies the biblical revelation to the contemporary social crisis by presenting the implications of the total gospel message for every area of life. Fundamentalism has often failed to do this.

Christian laymen, like theologians and statesmen, are also becoming increasingly aware that the answer to the many problems of political, industrial, and social life is a theological one. They are looking to the Christian church for guidance, and they are looking for a demonstration of the fact that the gospel of Jesus Christ is a transforming and vital force. We have the conviction that consecrated and gifted evangelical scholarship can provide concrete proof and strategic answers.

Christianity Today is cognizant of the dissolving effect of modern scientific theory upon religion. To counteract this tendency, it sets forth the unity of the divine revelation in nature and Scripture.

Three years in a theological seminary is not sufficient to prepare a student fully for the ministry. *Christianity Today* seeks to supplement seminary training with sermonic helps, pastoral advice, and book reviews, by leading ministers and scholars.

The interpretation of the news becomes more and more important in the present world situation. Correspondents conversant with local conditions have been enlisted in the United States and abroad. Through their reports *Christianity Today* seeks to provide its readers with a comprehensive and relevant view of religious movements and life throughout the world.

While affirming the great emphases of the historic creeds, the magazine seeks to avoid controversial denominational differences. It does not intend to concern itself with personalities or with purely internal problems and conflicts of the various denominations, though, if significant enough, these are objectively reported.

Into an era of unparalleled problems and opportunities for the church comes *Christianity Today* with the firm conviction that the historic evangelical faith is vital for the life of the church and of the nations. We believe that the gospel is still the power of God unto salvation for all who believe; that the basic needs of the social order must meet their solution first in the redemption of the individual; that the church and the individual Christian do have a vital responsibility to be both salt and light in a decaying and darkening world.

Believing that a great host of true Christians, whose faith has been impaired, are today earnestly seeking for a faith to live by and a message to proclaim, *Christianity Today* continues to dedicate itself to the presentation of the reasonableness and effectiveness of the Christian evangel. This we undertake with sincere Christian love for those who may differ with us, and with whom we may be compelled to differ, and with the assurance in our hearts that God's Holy Spirit alone can activate any vital witness for him.

24

EVANGELICALISM TODAY

We have seen a number of significant changes on the American church scene in the past several decades. Not least among them is the emergence of evangelicalism as the most significant religious movement throughout the world, as well as in America. You could almost say that its growth has been explosive and that its force continues to increase.

I'm grateful for the evangelical resurgence we've seen across the world in the last half-century or more. It truly has been God's doing. It wasn't like this when I first started preaching, and I'm amazed at what has happened. Along with this resurgence of evangelicalism has come the emergence of large numbers of evangelicals taking strong political positions. Whatever the future holds for such movements, they have probably already made a historic impact on American life.

I see two other marks of evangelical resurgence that I want to discuss in more detail. The first is the rise of a new ecumenism, and the second is a new emphasis on evangelism.

A New Vision for Ecumenism

This new emphasis on the unity of the body of Christ, or at least, a broader understanding and cooperative attitude between denominations, shows itself in several ways. I will mention three of them.

The Growing Understanding between Roman Catholics and Protestants

Just a few decades ago Catholics and Protestants could hardly speak with each other openly. In the last several years of our crusades, however, thousands of Catholics felt free to attend. I have preached in Roman Catholic schools and have even received honorary doctorates from them. This could not have happened twenty-five years ago.

In 2004 I spent about a half-hour with Pope John Paul II in a very private, intimate conversation. He was extremely warm and interested in our work. I had just been to Poland, and of course he wanted to know my impressions. We discussed the Christian faith, both our agreements and some of our differences. I had great admiration for the pope's moral courage.

That meeting with the pope helped our meetings in Mexico, because Catholics felt free to attend them. They saw that I was not a bigot or intolerant. Things are changing rapidly in Latin America. The differences between Protestants and Catholics remain very deep and very great, but in many instances, the two groups are at least beginning to talk to each other.

One helpful trend I see in the Catholic Church is a move toward greater diversity. Many of the diversities we have seen within Protestantism are now evident in Roman Catholicism. In fact, many Roman Catholics see fragmentation as a great danger. On the practical side, many Catholics in many parts of the world are rediscovering the Scriptures in a very real way. I also sense an openness to new approaches, including borrowing music and methods we have been familiar with in evangelical circles. When I was at the Vatican, I spoke at vespers at the North American College, which is a seminary for students from North America. I understand I was the first Protestant to speak there. It was a very inspirational and Christocentric service, with much contemporary music.

Evangelicals and the Charismatic Movement

The words *Holy Spirit* and *Pentecost* no longer belong exclusively to the so-called Pentecostal denominations. The charismatic impact is now widespread among many denominations, including the more liturgical churches.

The charismatic movement also has brought together in a new way Christians from various backgrounds and persuasions. Of course, there have been extremists in some places who have given it a bad name. I am encouraged to see many charismatic leaders stressing the need for deeper Bible study and balanced biblical doctrine. By and large, the charismatic movement has been a positive force in the lives of many people.

Evangelical Resurgence in the Mainline Denominations

There are more evangelicals in mainline denominations now than there were thirty years ago, especially among laymen. Evangelical seminaries have grown greatly and are full, whereas, on the whole, the more liberal ones do not have as many students. Students from the more evangelical seminaries increasingly are filling pulpits in many denominations. Surprising statements are now coming from many denominational leaders who are admitting they must take a closer, more sympathetic look at the evangelical revival.

Considering all these developments, we must take seriously our Lord's prayer in John 17, "that they may be one as we are one" (17:11 NIV1984). Someone has said the closer we get to Christ, the closer we get to each other. But already there is an ecumenism throughout the Christian world. Everyone who truly knows Christ is a member of the body of Christ—regardless of denominational label. When our Lord spoke through John to the seven churches of Asia, he rebuked them for their sins, but he did not tell them all to join the same church. I have no problems working with anyone, under any label, as long as he knows the Lord Jesus Christ as his Savior and is living the life of a Christian disciple.

There is far more agreement among evangelicals today than possibly at any time in my lifetime. There are, perhaps, some differences on social and political questions that are more evident today because of our visibility. The pendulum swings back and forth on some of the social, economic, and political issues. But most evangelicals recognize they have responsibilities in these areas in certain contexts. I have been called "liberal" in some areas because of my stand on certain social issues; I have been called "conservative" theologically. I accept both labels and believe that I stand in the mainstream of evangelicalism.

THE CURRENT EMPHASIS ON EVANGELISM

In 1960 a small group came together in Montreux, Switzerland, to discuss the possibility of unity among evangelicals. After listening to several days of discussion and debate—and after much time together in prayer—I became convinced that evangelicals would never get together except around one word: *evangelism.* That was the beginning of seed thoughts that led to the 1966 Berlin Congress, which in turn led to many regional congresses on evangelism (such as Amsterdam, Bogota, Singapore, Minneapolis), and later the 1974 Lausanne Congress on World Evangelism.

Of course, evangelism has always been dear to my heart. God called me to one particular segment of the field where the seed is to be sown—what people call mass evangelism. But not all evangelism must be on a mass basis. God has raised up scores of methods of evangelism that are very successful, probably more successful than ours. But the concept of crusade evangelism has also been used of God. Often a great deal happens as a result of crusades, far beyond the immediate meetings. Dr. Robert Evans once told me that he had uncovered more than twenty-five evangelical organizations in Europe alone that started as a direct or indirect result of our crusades in Europe.

I remember when the Lord opened up a whole new ministry of evangelism for us. After one of our telecasts, we tested call-ins for spiritual counseling and had counselors standing by in three cities. With our limited number of phones and counselors, we were able to talk to over one thousand people on each of four nights; many thousands more attempted to call. An average of 375 made commitments to Christ each evening. We did not have a toll-free number—people had to pay for their own calls. It was an indication to me that there was a far greater spiritual hunger among the American people than crusade reports indicated.

I am glad to see evangelicals working on methods for reaching people. I have said that the world won't be won from a stadium. In my judgment, there is no such thing as mass evangelism—that is a misnomer. If you speak to two people, you are speaking to a group. There is no more effective method than one-on-one. All so-called mass evangelism must be built on a foundation of one-on-one evangelism to be effective.

SHORTCOMINGS OF TODAY'S EVANGELICALS

While we have much to rejoice about in the current resurgence of evangelicalism, we evangelicals also have a few shortcomings that we need to address.

Individualism

Among these has been an unhealthy tendency toward individualism—a tendency on the part of some individualists to go their own way. Also, I think we have failed to communicate to the world church some of the positive things evangelicals are doing, such as in the area of social work. I have also been concerned because too often we have tended toward superficiality—an overemphasis on easy-believism or experience rather than on true discipleship. We have sometimes offered cheap grace and cheap conversions without genuine repentance. In addition, evangelicals have not tried to capture the intellectual initiative as much as we should.

> We have sometimes offered cheap grace and cheap conversions without genuine repentance.

We haven't challenged and developed the minds of our generation. Though there are many exceptions, generally we evangelicals have failed to present to the world great thinkers, theologians, artists, scientists, and so forth.

Materialism

Materialism and affluence have adversely affected evangelicals in America. On the positive side, our relative affluence has meant we have been able to support missionaries and ministries in many parts of the world. On the negative side, we have sometimes become too preoccupied with our lifestyle, both as individuals and as organizations. The Bible speaks of "the deceitfulness of wealth" (Matthew 13:22 NIV 1984) and how it chokes the Word in our lives. Many of the great people of the Bible (like Abraham or David) had great wealth, but God was first in their lives. It is a person's attitude toward his affluence that makes the difference. God has raised up throughout the years wealthy individuals who see their riches as a stewardship from God—men like Count Zinzendorf, Lord Shaftesbury, and Lord Dartmouth, who gave George Whitefield money for his evangelistic work.

Of course, affluence is a relative thing. Someone we might consider impoverished may be looked upon as wealthy in his own culture. An Indian, for example, who may be getting $600 a year, is considered wealthy by Bangladesh standards, where the average income may be $50 or $100 a year. But I believe those of us in the affluent countries must move toward a more simple lifestyle, because we are citizens of the world community and the world church.

This was a concern throughout our whole organization. We all felt a simpler lifestyle was God's way for us. Several years ago my wife and I got rid of some of the things that we may have held too closely.

We evangelicals must not expect that following Christ will make our lives easy. I do not agree with those who say our lives should be trouble-free if we are following Christ. Each of us faces problems—an illness, a family problem, an economic reversal—and we need to prepare for those times now by learning to live without more of what we could so easily lose. Also, we need to realize that God can bring great blessing to us through suffering and difficulties.

The most important thing we can do is grow in our relationship to Christ. If we have not learned to pray in our everyday lives, we will find it difficult to know God's peace and strength through prayer when the hard times come. If we have not learned to trust God's Word when times are easy, we will not trust his Word when we face difficulties. I am convinced that one of the greatest things we can do is to memorize Scripture. The Scriptures speak to us in those moments when we look to the Lord for sustenance and strength.

Impersonal Churches

Another downside for evangelicals is that churches can be too large and impersonal. They are not really able to minister to their members. Many illustrations of this have come to my attention. There are church members who tell us they can't get to their pastor or another person on the staff. Recently a man told me that he had been going to his church for over a year. He said, "I don't believe there are five people there who know my name." That is a tragedy. Of course, some large churches have broken the congregation into smaller groups, so that all the people may be ministered to personally.

Somewhere along the line we need to study carefully how many people a clergyman can minister to. Clergymen are among the most susceptible to nervous breakdowns, and even to attacks of Satan, simply because they are too busy to take time for their devotional life and their families. In many churches we probably need to learn more about the ministry of the laity. The minister shouldn't be doing everything; he should "prepare God's people for works of service, so that the body of Christ may be built up" (Ephesians 4:12 NIV).

I have a friend who is the pastor of a large Presbyterian church. When he went there, he told the elders that his family came first. There would be times when he would be gone, he said, and he didn't want them asking where. He has a marvelous Christian family, which is a great witness for him.

Theological Illiteracy

Another thing that bothers me terribly—as much as anything I can think of—is that so many evangelicals seem to be theologically illiterate. One of the great needs in America is Bible teaching in depth. Unless this happens, I fear we will see many distortions and errors creeping into evangelicalism in the future. I think, incidentally, that *Christianity Today* can have an important role here.

Imposing Christian Morality

One shortcoming that I think few evangelicals are aware of is their expectation that the world will live by Christian standards. We cannot take our Christian values and force them on the world. Christians have to realize that, morally, we live in a different world.

If an unmarried girl who is living with a man and really enjoying it came to me wondering what was wrong with it, I would tell the young lady—if she were not a Christian—that from a long-term psychological point of view she is making a tragic mistake. From the standpoint of a future marital relationship, I would tell her that what the Scriptures teach is for her best. For example, how can there be real trust and security in a married relationship, or any lasting commitment, if marriage is not taken seriously?

On the other hand, if she were a Christian girl, I would tell her frankly that she is sinning. It is displeasing to God. Our fellowship with him is broken when we tolerate sin in our lives.

We evangelicals cannot single out one sin from the scores mentioned in Scripture and ride a hobbyhorse—although I have had a lot of pressure across the years to do so. There is a difference between sin and sins. There is *sin* (singular), which is the heart of our spiritual disease, and there are *sins* (plural), which are the fruit or signs of the disease. If I spent all of my time on *sins* (plural) I might never be able to get at the root cause, which is *sin* (singular). The Lord Jesus Christ died on the cross to deal with *sin*, and not just individual *sins*.

THE MOST IMPORTANT ISSUE
FACING EVANGELICALS

The most important issue we face today is the same the church has faced in every century: Will we reach our world for Christ? In other words, will we give priority to Christ's command to go into all the world and preach the gospel? Or will we turn increasingly inward, caught up in our own internal affairs or controversies, simply becoming more and more comfortable with the status quo? Will we become inner-directed or outer-directed? The central issues of our time aren't economic or political or social, important as these are. The central issues of our time are moral and spiritual in nature, and our calling is to declare Christ's forgiveness and hope and transforming power to a world that does not know him or follow him. May we never forget this.

25

MY ROLE IN THE
WATERGATE CRISIS

When President Nixon asked me to hold a Christmas service in the White House on December 16, 1974, I realized the delicacy of such a visit in the Watergate climate. I recognized also, however, the responsibility of such a service and the opportunity to present the gospel of Christ within a Christmas context to a distinguished audience. I had said for many years that I would go anywhere to preach the gospel, whether to the Vatican, the Kremlin, or the White House, if there were no strings on what I was to say. I never had to submit a manuscript to the White House or get anybody's approval. I never informed any president of what I was going to say ahead of time. They all knew that when I came, I intended to preach the gospel. I am first and foremost a servant of Jesus Christ.

My first allegiance is not to America but to the kingdom of God.

Some criticized this kind of involvement with President Nixon. That view was ridiculous. In the 1950s we called such thinking "McCarthyism"—guilt by association. This was the accusation of the Pharisees against Jesus, that he spent time with "publicans and sinners." Through the years I stated publicly that I did not agree with all that any administration did. I certainly did not agree with everything that President Johnson did, and I was at the White House as often under Johnson as under Nixon. I preached before Johnson more than I preached before Nixon and had longer and more frequent conversations with him. But I did not agree with everything Johnson did. I publicly stated so on several occasions.

On one of those occasions I think he was irritated with me, but he soon got over it. After that, I tried to make it a point, which I am sure was obscured and blurred, that I went to the White House to preach the gospel and that my preaching visits had absolutely nothing to do with the current political situation. It was quite obvious that I did not agree with everything the Nixon administration did.

I can make no excuses for Watergate. The actual break-in was a criminal act, and some of the things that surrounded Watergate, too, were not only unethical but criminal. I condemn it and I deplore it. It hurt America.

Responding to My Critics

Some evangelicals wondered why I did not go to the White House like Nathan the prophet and censure the president publicly. Let's remember that I was not a "Nathan." David was the leader of "the people of God," which made it a totally different situation than what we have in today's secularistic America. A better comparison would be with ancient Rome and Paul's relationship with Caesar. Also, when a pastor has in his congregation a mayor or a governor who may be in some difficulty, he doesn't point this man out publicly from the pulpit. He tries to encourage and help him and to lead him. Perhaps in private he will advise him on the moral and spiritual implications of the situation, but I don't think the average clergyman in the pulpit would take advantage of such a situation and point to this man and say publicly, "You ought to do thus and so."

If I had had anything to say to the president, it would have been in private. When you have the confidence of a public official and he tells you things in private, if you ever once break that trust, you'll never again have that opportunity, with him or with anyone else. I don't think that clergymen should go around telling private conversations any more than a psychiatrist or a private attorney or a doctor should. We clergymen should certainly have as high ethics as the medical profession—in fact, much higher.

Some have cited the example of Ambrose of Milan, who publicly rebuked the emperor Theodosius when he came to church. Ambrose refused to let the emperor inside until he had made a public confession of certain wrongs. But that's not a proper parallel either, though I greatly admire Ambrose for his courage. Ambrose was a political as well as a religious figure. I was not a bishop, as was Ambrose, nor was President Nixon my subject, as was Theodosius. I had no ecclesiastical power over him. I think the president comes into the church with the same status as anyone else: either as a sinner saved by God's grace or a sinner in need of that grace.

> *I think the president comes into the church with the same status as anyone else: either as a sinner saved by God's grace or a sinner in need of that grace.*

Some criticized my involvement with President Nixon, saying the White House was making me a tool to influence people who would be impressed by seeing the president at prayer or listening to a sermon. That's foolish. Did President Kennedy make a tool of Cardinal Cushing? Of course not. If Mr. Nixon wanted to make me a tool, why did he cease to invite me to the White House during the period when he might have needed a person like me the most?

Twice in the year when the Watergate crisis was hottest, I offered to talk to the president. One of his aides said that one of the reasons Mr. Nixon didn't have me was that he didn't want to hurt me. Now whether that's true or not, I don't know, but I remember in 1960 when he was running for president, there was a rumor that I might endorse him. He called and told me not to endorse him if I was thinking of it. He said, "Billy, your ministry is more important than my election to the presidency."

PREACHERS AND PRESIDENTS

Many presidents have had close relationships with clergymen. I would say that my relationship with Mr. Nixon was not as close as that between other presidents and clergymen of their day. One example was the relationship between John R. Mott, called the architect of the ecumenical movement, and President Woodrow Wilson. Wilson went to Mott for advice and counsel not only on religious matters but also on political and diplomatic matters. I don't think people credited or blamed Mott for what went on in the Wilson administration.

I also don't think people held Cardinal Cushing accountable during the Kennedy administration. And he certainly was with the Kennedys a great deal more than I was with Mr. Nixon. Cardinal Cushing acted as a pastor to the Kennedy family. He might have given political advice privately. I knew Cardinal Cushing quite well, and I know that he wasn't above giving a political word here and there. Throughout the years I have said things to various presidents that could be construed as political advice. I'm not too quick anymore to make political judgments.

Many politicians and media people thought Mr. Nixon might have weathered his crisis better had he been willing to admit that he made a mistake. I won't reveal what I said to him privately, but I have personally found that when you have made a mistake, it's far better to admit it. I've had to admit errors in judgment, and I've found Christian people more than generous in understanding my faults. I think they would try to understand any president's position, too. It's better to show humility, and it's better to say "I'm wrong" or "I'm sorry" when you've made a mistake.

The Bible says, "Thou shalt not bear false witness" (Exodus 20:16). That commandment has never been rescinded, and lying is wrong no matter who does it.

NIXON THE MAN

We must remember that President Nixon or any president is only a human being. He was finite, and no president I have ever met considered himself really big enough for the job, especially after the first year. I don't think there was even a White House press corps until McKinley's administration, and then there was only one reporter. All of this tends to drive a president into some isolationism in order to live with himself, think a little, read a little, and spend some time with his family.

However, I have to speak about the Nixon I knew before he became president. To me, he was always a warm and gracious person with a great sense of humor. He was always thoughtful. Sometimes I was with him when he was preoccupied, but I never had the impression that he was cold or diffident. Of course, other people knew him better than I did and knew him in a different way.

I always admired Nixon's close family life. I admired his love for his mother, his wife, and their daughters. I admired his tremendous passion for peace, which I think came partly from his Quaker background. I also admired his personal discipline. I've known few men that lived such a disciplined life. He once told me that the reason he gave up golf was that there were too many books to read and too many interesting conversations to hold. He said, "I may never be elected president but I'm going to continue preparing myself."

That brings up another interesting point. During 1967 and early 1968 he really did not want to run for president. He almost decided not to. He was actually afraid that something like what finally happened to him might indeed occur. I think his running for president came partially as a result of ambition but mostly as a result of sheer patriotism. He really felt he could make a contribution—not only to America but to the world, especially in foreign affairs. He seemed to feel the midseventies would be very dangerous for America and the world.

WHY DID WATERGATE OCCUR?

I think Mr. Nixon and his men had what I would call a "magnificent obsession" to change the country and the world. A year before he decided to run for president, he listed to me point by point what he thought ought to be done. One thing was to end the Cold War. He also wanted to balance the budget. Another goal was to control crime, which was growing rampant at about that time. And another one was ending the Vietnam War. This was his number-one concern, and I think he really thought he could end Vietnam much quicker than he did.

The Nixon aides thought his reelection was the most important thing in the world. They thought that future peace depended on him. I think most of them were very sincere, but they began to rationalize that the end justified the means, even if it meant taking liberties with law and the truth. They had seen the law broken by people who had other causes. They had heard people call for all kinds of civil disobedience. They felt that their cause was just as great as peace in Vietnam and civil rights. In fact, they felt peace in Vietnam could only be achieved by the re-election of Mr. Nixon. Many of these men were very young. In fact, President Nixon had the youngest staff in the history of the White House.

In addition, I think the president himself was so occupied with détente with the Soviet Union and China and giving so much time and thought to it that he gave little thought to his re-election campaign. I think he was so sure of his election that he just left it to other people. Perhaps that was part of the problem.

The Christian Response to Governmental Wrongdoing

If God is God, then what God says must be absolute—man must have moral boundaries. He cannot devise his own morals to fit his own situation. The Bible tells us that with what judgment we judge we shall be judged. So we must avoid hypocritical and self-righteous glee at the evil that has been done. The Bible also teaches us, "Lie not one to another" (Colossians 3:9). There is no blinking at the fact that Watergate became a symbol of political corruption and evil. But let us realize that there is one crisis more urgent than all other crises that America has faced, and that is the crisis in integrity and in Christian love and in forgiveness.

In countries where there is a state-church relationship, people don't necessarily hold the church or church leaders responsible for all the political decisions. I never quite understood why I was considered in some way responsible for or part of any administration, whether under Presidents Johnson, Nixon, Clinton, or the two Bush presidents. I just happened to be friends with them. We should guard against guilt by association.

I was never considered President Nixon's pastor. He had several friends among the clergy. I was more a personal family friend than a pastor. I actually met Mr. Nixon in the early 1950s through his father and mother. They had attended my meetings in southern California. When a friend is down, you don't go and kick him—you try to help him up.

We must remember that the Christian has one primary duty to those in authority, whether they are right or wrong, good or bad: to pray! "I exhort therefore, that, first of all, supplications, prayers, intercessions, and giving of thanks, be made for all men; for kings, and for all that are in authority; that we may lead a quiet and peaceable life in all godliness and honesty" (1 Timothy 2:1–2).

26

WHAT I WOULD
HAVE DONE DIFFERENTLY

One of my great regrets is that I have not studied enough. I wish I had studied more and preached less. People pressured me into speaking to groups when I should have been studying and preparing. Donald Barnhouse said that if he knew the Lord was coming in three years, he would spend two of them studying and one preaching.

If I had it to do over again, I would try to organize my time much better. I took too many speaking engagements in too many places around the world. I would not speak less in the great stadiums; I would speak less at all kinds of conferences and events that I was invited to throughout the world, especially in Great Britain and the United States. I'd travel to those places, and I didn't have time to think and study and pray. And I needed time for that. Also, I did not spend enough time with my family when they were growing up. You cannot recapture those years.

I might add here that through the years I met many, many people. Yet I feel terrible that I could not keep up with all those friends and acquaintances.

I did some things that I probably didn't really need to do either—weddings and funerals and building dedications, things like that. Whenever I counsel someone who feels called to be an evangelist, I always urge him to guard his time and not feel like he has to do everything.

I also would have steered clear of politics. I'm grateful for the opportunities God gave me to minister to people in high places; people in power have spiritual and personal needs like everyone else, and often they have no one to talk to. But looking back I know I sometimes crossed the line, and I wouldn't do that now.

If I had it to do over again, I'd spend more time in meditation and prayer and just telling the Lord how much I love and adore him and looking forward to the time we're going to spend together for eternity.

Part Six
THE
GRAHAM LEGACY

27

THE HUMILITY OF GREATNESS

By John R. W. Stott

*John R. W. Stott (1921–2011) first met Billy Graham in the 1940s, while shar-
ing an open-air meeting at Speaker's Corner in London's Hyde Park. Their shared
concern for evangelism led to a close association during Graham's 1954 Harringay Crusade, which captivated London nightly for nearly three months. Over the
next fifty years the two men's lives would frequently intertwine, through shared
leadership in significant ventures like Lausanne's International Congress on World
Evangelization, and in personal friendship. Stott offered these reminiscences before he died.*

*I*ntegrity. If I had to choose one word with which to characterize
Billy Graham, it would be *integrity*. He was all of a piece. There was
no dichotomy between what he said and what he was. He practiced
what he preached. Here are some examples:

Finance. When Billy Graham first came to London, he met a con-
siderable group of church leaders who were wondering whether to in-

vite him to come. They were critical, but he had anticipated their questions. He was able to say that he received a fixed salary, less than most salaries paid to the senior pastors of large churches, and he received no "love offerings" (unaccounted extras). As for crusade finances, they were published in the press each crusade.

Sex. Billy Graham was exemplary in his private life—obviously in love with Ruth. Sometimes he said publicly that he had slept with one woman only throughout his life, and that was his wife, Ruth. He had no skeletons in any cupboard.

Harringay. After the close of the Harringay Crusade was postponed, it went on to last twelve weeks and was a remarkable phenomenon. Our church (All Souls Langham Place) was fully involved and I went almost every night. Night after night twelve thousand people assembled and listened attentively to the message. And night after night I asked myself what brought the crowds when many of our churches were half-full and therefore half-empty. And the answer I gave myself was that Billy Graham was the first transparently sincere preacher they had ever heard. There was something authentic about that man. As many media people confessed, "We don't agree with him, but we know he is sincere."

Courage. Few Christian leaders (if any) have had the opportunity that Billy had to be granted an audience with successive presidents of the U.S., with Queen Elizabeth II in the U.K., and with many other national leaders. Lesser mortals than Graham might well have used such opportunities to boost their own ego, but Billy used them as opportunities for the gospel. He was not afraid of human beings, however exalted in the opinion of humans.

Study. Billy Graham was always conscious of not having had a formal theological education. But he had a substantial personal library and kept up some regular reading. Speaking to about six hundred clergy in London in November 1979, Graham said that if he had his ministry all over again he would make two changes; people looked startled. What could he possibly mean? First, he continued, he would study three times as much as he had done. He would take on fewer engagements. "I've preached too much," he went on, "and studied too little." The second change he would make was that he would give more time to prayer. In making these statements, he must have had the two apostolic priorities of Acts 6:4 in mind.

Christmas 1956. In November 1955 I had the privilege of serving as Billy Graham's "Chief Assistant Missioner" during his Cambridge University Mission. During those ten days our friendship strengthened, and I was touched to be invited later to spend Christmas with the family at Montreat. I cherish two most vivid memories of those days. The first was family prayers each day. I saw the world-famous evangelist reading the Scripture and praying with Ruth and their children. Secondly, we were all given Christmas parcels which we carried to a settlement of poor "hillbilly" families in the mountains nearby. Again, Graham the mass evangelist was to be seen sharing the gospel with small groups.

Message. I would oversimplify by drawing attention to two characteristics. The first was his continual return to the good news of Christ crucified. He was constantly criticized but, though he listened to criticism, he refused to allow criticism to dislodge him from his essential gospel. Secondly, he read several newspapers and had aides scouring them for him. So he was always commenting relevantly on the latest news.

> *He was constantly criticized but, though he listened to criticism, he refused to allow criticism to dislodge him from his essential gospel.*

Social Conscience. Billy Graham accepted the statements of the Lausanne Covenant, which stated that we are called to both social action and evangelism. Although he knew that his personal vocation was to serve as an evangelist, he had the courage in South Africa to refuse to be involved in a crusade in which apartheid regulations operated. He also had a personally tender social conscience and supported many good causes of a social nature.

Influence. He did much (especially through the Amsterdam conference) to encourage younger evangelists. He put evangelism on the ecclesiastical map, making it respectable in a new way. But his influence is perhaps best seen in a new worldwide evangelical unity, manifest in such initiatives as the launching of *Christianity Today* and the congresses: worldwide (Lausanne 1974, Manila 1989, Cape Town 2010), national, and regional.

Team. A notable feature of the Billy Graham Evangelistic Association is that it was never a one-man show. True, Billy was always the main preacher, though Grady Wilson did a lot until he died. But the trio of Billy, Cliff Barrows, and Bev Shea, dating from their school days, was remarkable. No traces of jealousy spoiled this cooperation. They evidently appreciated one another and supported one another.

28

GRAHAM THE BRIDGE BUILDER

By Richard John Neuhaus

Richard John Neuhaus (1936–2009) was founder and editor of the journal First Things. *First a prominent Lutheran pastor, then a Roman Catholic priest, he was a significant figure in evangelical-Catholic relations and coauthored* Evangelicals and Catholics Together *with Charles Colson. He prepared this tribute to Graham before his own death in 2009.*

The courage required for Billy Graham to open his southern crusades to blacks and the courage to cooperate with Roman Catholics—both measures vigorously criticized by many of his supporters—was not courage of the kind conventionally lauded as liberal or progressive. It is true that challenging racial segregation and anti-Catholic prejudice were both deemed to be progressive stances, but I am rather sure that carried little weight with Billy Graham. His singular passion was to preach the saving gospel of Jesus Christ to absolutely everyone.

Many Catholic leaders warmly welcomed his ministry; others were more ambivalent. Here in New York, the late John Cardinal O'Connor embraced him and urged the priests of the archdiocese to encourage people to come out to hear him. There can be no doubt that innumerable Catholics were renewed and strengthened in faith as a consequence of the ministry of Billy Graham.

He met with popes from John XXIII to John Paul II, and his friendship with the latter seemed to be especially warm and deep. In an extraordinary personal meeting of two hours in 1989, Graham reported, "There was a pause in the conversation; suddenly the pope's arm shot out and he grabbed the lapels of my coat. He pulled me forward within inches of his own face. He fixed his eyes on me and said, 'Listen Graham, we are brothers.'"

Already in 1966, only a year after the Second Vatican Council, Graham said, "I find myself closer to Catholics than the radical Protestants. I think the Roman Catholic Church today is going through a second Reformation." On the *Phil Donahue Show* in 1979, he said, "I think the American people are looking for a leader, a moral and spiritual leader that believes something. And the pope does. . . . Thank God, I've got somebody to quote now with some real authority." On John Paul's visit to America in 1980: "Since his election, Pope John Paul II has emerged as the greatest religious leader of the modern world, and one of the greatest moral and spiritual leaders of this century. . . . The pope came [to America] as a statesman and a pastor, but I believe he also sees himself coming as an evangelist. . . . The pope sought to speak to the spiritual hunger of our age in the same way

Christians throughout the centuries have spoken to the spiritual yearnings of every age—by pointing people to Christ." And, later, on the pope's message in Vancouver, where Graham preached a month later: "I'll tell you, that was just about as straight an evangelical address as I've ever heard. It was tremendous. Of course, I'm a great admirer of his. He gives moral guidance in a world that seems to have lost its way."

In his statements about John Paul II, as well as about Mother Teresa and the Catholic Church more generally, many evangelicals thought Graham had gone overboard, while others claimed he had landed in gross heresy. But I am confident that what he said and felt was driven by a passion for sharing the saving gospel of Christ. In the great encyclical of 2000, *Redemptoris Missio* (Mission of the Redeemer), John Paul envisioned the third millennium as "a springtime of world evangelization." The entirety of Billy Graham's life was surrendered to playing some part, however small, in precipitating that springtime. Those of us who believe there is such a springtime know that his part was not small.

In a world Christian movement of more than two billion people, more than half of them Roman Catholic, he understood that such a springtime would require "Evangelicals and Catholics Together." He declined to sign the first statement by that title issued in 1994. The reason, as it was explained to me, was, first, that he had a general rule of not signing group statements and, second, that ECT was at the time receiving harsh criticism from some evangelicals and he feared his signing could be divisive. Of the several statements produced by ECT over the years, the most important single affirmation was contained in the first: "Evangelicals and Catholics are brothers and sisters in Christ." Everything else follows from that, and I have no doubt that Billy Graham joined in that affirmation.

There are many things that might be said about Graham's impact on American Catholicism. In the larger historical perspective, perhaps the most interesting is his part in reconfiguring the location of Catholicism in the American experience. America has been and still is a predominantly Protestant country, not only in numbers but in a spiritual tradition that runs from Jonathan Edwards in the eighteenth century through the several awakenings and crusading evangelists of whom, it might be argued, Billy Graham was the greatest.

Over three centuries, Catholic leaders generally assumed that Catholics would secure their place in the American experience by cooperation with the Protestant liberal mainline that is now in such sad theological, moral, and institutional disarray. By its very nature, Catholicism must try to remain in constructive conversation with everyone, but it seems increasingly evident that the future really is one of evangelicals and Catholics together. Scholars who attempt to explain how this came about will have to pay major attention to the person and ministry of Billy Graham. As we Catholics say, *Requiescat in pace*, and may choirs of angels greet him on the far side of Jordan.

29

GROWING UP "GRAHAM"

By Ruth Graham

Ruth Graham is the third (and youngest) daughter of Billy and Ruth Graham.
She is author of In Every Pew Sits a Broken Heart *as well as* A Legacy of
Faith: Things I Learned from My Father.

Everybody always asks, "What was it like to grow up being Billy
Graham's kid?" Well, this is my answer.

Growing up I didn't see a lot of him. But I kept every letter, every
note, every scrap. I even carry his signature in my wallet. Going back
through them, I saw his letters of love and advice. He may have been
in Africa, but he would write in longhand, four pages—long pages—
just giving me advice, encouragement.

One principle he passed down to me is depending on God. I
started my own ministry [Ruth Graham & Friends] and asked him,
"Daddy, did you ever feel inadequate or intimidated?" And he said,
"Oh, yes, all the time." I said, "How did you prepare for that?" He

said, "I prayed." The next morning, I said, "Daddy, what was your prayer?" I was looking for a formula. And he said, "I would sit in the rocker in the mountain cabin, and I prayed by the hour, 'Lord, help,' and, 'Holy Spirit, fill me.'" Simple. Everybody has access to that.

After my failed second marriage, I had to go home. My parents had previously warned me, "Don't do this." Daddy had even called me from Tokyo to tell me to slow down, but I was headstrong and married anyway. It wasn't long before I realized I'd made a terrible mistake. And I had to flee. I packed up what I could in my car and started for home. It was a two-day drive. Questions swirled in my mind. What were my parents going to say to me? "You've made your bed; now lie in it." "We're tired of dealing with you." Were they going to accept me or reject me? The guilt and the shame built with every mile. As I rounded the last bend in my parents' driveway, my father was standing there. As I got out of the car, he wrapped his arms around me and said, "Welcome home." That's grace.

Not long before Mother died, I was talking to Mother and Daddy around the dinner table about dealing with one of my children, who was driving me nuts. My father was quite deaf, and I didn't think he was paying attention, and Mother was giving me advice. As he turned to leave the room, he called me to him. "Ruth," he said, "she's trying to do the right thing. You need to support her." Grace.

I'm much more warmed by the embers than I ever was by the

fire. My father mellowed over the years. His softness and his gentleness came out. He was so dear. Calvin Thielman, who was our pastor in Montreat for years, said, "The older you get, the more like yourself you become." My father became this gentle, kind, thoughtful, gracious man.

30

MORE THAN A ROLE MODEL

By Tullian Tchividjian

Tullian Tchividjian is senior pastor of Coral Ridge Presbyterian Church in Ft. Lauderdale, Florida, and son of Virginia (Gigi) Graham.

It was May 2, 1996, and I was sitting in the U.S. Capitol rotunda with my family, anticipating the ceremony about to begin. I had been to Washington, D.C., once before, in 1985, when I was just thirteen years old. This trip was different, though. We were there because my grandparents were being honored with the Congressional Gold Medal, the highest honor the Congress of the United States can bestow on a citizen. In fact, Senator Bob Dole, during a speech at the ceremony, said, "When the idea of awarding the Congressional Gold Medal to Billy and Ruth Graham was first raised, it received something rare in this building—unanimous approval." Everybody laughed. At the time, it was the 114th medal awarded, with George Washington being the first recipient.

Hundreds came that day to honor my grandparents, ranging from then–vice president Al Gore to Kathie Lee Gifford. When Newt Gingrich, Senator Dole, and Vice President Gore spoke, they each shared how much my grandparents meant to them personally.

After the medal was presented, my granddad got up to speak. Before he could say a word, the crowd stood and applauded for a solid three minutes. Tears began streaming down my face. I was so proud of him and so thankful that God had given me such a tremendous heritage, one I had neither asked for nor deserved. Here was a man being publicly honored for preaching the gospel of Jesus Christ to more people than anyone in history; a man being recognized for his love for God and love for others—and I had the privilege of calling him "Daddy Bill." As we all stood and clapped, I prayed: "Lord, no matter what it is that you call me to do, I want to do it with the God-centered focus, passion, and humility that have characterized the life and ministry of my grandfather."

It was no surprise that Daddy Bill presented the gospel that day. He spoke boldly of sin, the cross, and the great need for repentance. He spoke about the brevity of life and the fleeting pleasures of this world. He looked into the eyes of the many high-ranking political leaders present that day and challenged them to contemplate death and the life to come. He was so bold, so unashamed of the gospel, and so winsome. To this day, I'm not sure I have ever heard the truth spoken in love more effectively. I had heard him preach a thousand times before, but that time was particularly moving. I'll never forget that day.

As I reflect on this memorable occasion, it reminds me of what I loved most about Daddy Bill—those qualities I had the rare opportunity of observing in an up-close and personal way. Five come to mind immediately.

HIS HUMILITY

Daddy Bill was always keenly aware that God was God and he was not. He was conscious of his smallness and God's bigness, his imperfection and God's perfection. Not long ago, I told someone that it wasn't until I got older that I realized how well known and significant my grandfather was. This was mainly due to the fact that he never, ever projected himself to be more or less important than anyone else. I didn't think he was extraordinary because he didn't think he was extraordinary. I never once saw him "think of himself more highly than he ought" (Romans 12:3).

HIS LOVE FOR THE GOSPEL

Daddy Bill had a deep sense of his own sin, which led him to a deep love for his Savior. He exemplified the sweet reality that you can never know Christ as a great Savior until you first know yourself to be a great sinner. God's amazing grace always amazed him—and that amazes me!

HIS FAITHFULNESS

Although he had the opportunity to do many other things, he never wavered from God's call on his life to be an evangelist. He knew he wasn't a scholar or a theologian, and he never pretended to be (although his friendships with Carl Henry, Harold Lindsell, Kenneth Kantzer, John Stott, and J. I. Packer testified to his respect for theologians and scholars). He remained true to God's calling on his life. And he fulfilled that calling without any taint of sexual, financial, or other moral scandal. He kept the main thing the main thing.

> *He kept the main thing the main thing.*

HE DIDN'T SHOW FAVORITISM

I was with Daddy Bill in many places at many times with many different people, and I never saw him show favoritism. He treated people the same, whether they were rich or poor, weak or powerful, socially significant or socially insignificant. Whenever we were in public and someone recognized him, he would stop and talk to them. Regardless of who it was, when he was talking to someone, there was no one more important to him at that moment than that person. Because of his belief that all people are made in God's image, he rightly concluded that there were no little people.

HIS HUMANNESS

Daddy Bill was normal! He got mad; he got sad; he got grumpy. He loved to laugh (especially at himself). He tended to be optimistic in public and pessimistic in private. His favorite restaurant was Red Lobster. His favorite movie was *Crocodile Dundee*. His favorite drink was orange juice, and he loved catfish. He was just another man with all of the limitations, imperfections, and idiosyncratic tastes that the rest of us have—and I loved him for it!

In the acknowledgments of my book *Do I Know God?*, I wrote: "To Daddy Bill for writing the foreword. I can't believe the heritage God has given me. Because of your faithfulness to Jesus for more than sixty years, my children and my children's children will be blessed. You have been one of my closest friends and most reliable counselors all my life. I want to be just like you when I grow up."

I miss you terribly, Daddy Bill. But as you always told me, "For the Christian, the best is yet to come."

31

AN UNLIKELY FRIENDSHIP

By Tony Carnes

Tony Carnes, longtime senior news writer for Christianity Today, *is now editor and publisher of* A Journey through NYC Religions, *which documents every New York City house of worship.*

B illy Graham and Johnny Cash were best of friends, mutual confessors, and fishing buddies. Their wives, Ruth Bell and June Carter, were prayer partners. The two men could sit for hours in the same room without saying a word—Billy working on a book and Johnny on his songs. Once in a while, Johnny would interrupt and try out a song on Billy or ask a question about the Bible. At mealtimes the families would gather to pray, sing, and eat. Usually the subject moved quickly to family and friends, problems and challenges. Johnny always had a list of friends he wanted Billy to call, while Billy would ask Johnny for advice and prayer for his loved ones.

Billy and Johnny's connection originated with Billy's desire to connect with his son Franklin and the boy's teenage peers. Franklin says that even as a little boy, "I loved Johnny Cash's music." He recalls that in 1969, Billy called the governor of Tennessee to ask for help in setting up an appointment with Cash. Billy was observing his son slip into smoking, drinking, drugs, and girls. Franklin left one school after another, sometimes after being expelled. In his autobiography, *Just as I Am*, Billy explained that Franklin believed he was successfully hiding these things from his dad—"or so he thought," Billy wrote.

Both father and son later agreed that Billy had approached Cash with the goal of connecting with Franklin. "My favorite song was 'Ring of Fire,'" says Franklin. "Father wanted to connect to me by connecting to Johnny Cash." The elder Graham framed the matter in more global terms while visiting the singer's home near Nashville.

Cash told *Country Music* magazine that he was curious about why Graham had come to see him. Cash had only recently gotten off drugs, started attending church, and married June. "We had a big meal and we sat around and talked a long time. I kept waiting for him to say what he came to see me about." Graham said he just wanted to talk about music, a conversational topic Graham's friends might have found surprising coming from the evangelist.

Then Graham obliquely mentioned his real concern: "He said the kids were not going to church, that they were losing interest in religion, and he said he thought that the music had a lot to do with it, because there was nothing in the church house that they heard that they liked," Cash recalled. Graham admitted that the music in church sounded old. His own crusades mainly used older hymns. "The latest thing the kids can hear in the church is 'Bringing in the Sheaves' and 'How Great Thou Art,'" the evangelist told the singer.

By this time Graham seemed to have shrewdly read Cash as a man who liked a challenge and maintained his own spiritual direction by having his friends gather around to move him in the right direction through rough spots. Cash recalled how Graham pricked his interest: "He kind of challenged me to challenge others, to try to use what talent we have to write something inspiring." According to Steve Turner, a Christian journalist who began collaboration with Cash on an autobiography just before the singer's death in 2003, Cash was taken by this pastor who was as charismatic as Cash, yet was humble and quietly confident in God.

Cash had found a friend, confidant, and inspiration—a down-home boy like himself, but one who plowed his rows straight. "Well, first thing that happened," Cash described, "the night after [Graham] left, I wrote 'What Is Truth?' Just him coming to the house inspired me to write that, if you want to call it inspiration." Cash then talked to June about producing a film in Israel about Jesus. The singer also appeared at a crusade in Knoxville, Tennessee, in 1970, the first of his thirty crusade appearances.

TEAMING UP FOR THE GOSPEL

The evangelist was intrigued by Cash's honesty about his troubles and his faith, and how that honesty connected with the nonchurchgoing crowd. Graham invited Cash to his May 24, 1970, crusade in Knoxville, Tennessee, causing some concern among Graham's staff. "There was an uproar in Dad's organization," Franklin recalls. "It was like he had invited Elvis Presley!"

Billy told people that Johnny was the type of person he wanted to reach. Franklin describes his dad's thinking as a way to minister to Johnny while also reaching new people. "Daddy saw the type of people Johnny would bring. And Johnny and June themselves came knowing they would hear the gospel." Graham's music director, Cliff Barrows, said that he knew Cash was adding a new dimension to the crusades: "All the guys that drove pickups and were in the 'rough and ready' crowd would come. We could always count on a larger percentage of unconverted folks to come who needed the Lord."

At the Knoxville crusade Graham and Cash teamed up to meet the Jesus Revolution of the early 1970s. Graham preached on the Jesus who could revolutionize someone's life, while Cash testified to Jesus' power to bring him off drugs, which he said "ain't worth it." Cash was entering a new phase of spiritual depth. Before, Jesus was his lifesaver—now he started to see Jesus as someone who could mature him. He characterized this change as a move from careerism to ministry. "I've lived all my life for the devil up until now," the singer told church audiences, "and from here on I'm going to live it for the Lord." Although Cash partnered with a number of ministries and was pastored by Jimmy Lee of Nashville, his personal relationship with Graham continued to grow.

In a bit of Nashville legend, Graham did a cameo role reciting a

Bible verse in one of Johnny's songs, "The Preacher Said, 'Jesus Said.'" Cash was inspired by Graham and his wife to film the life of Christ in Israel. *The Gospel Road* was bought by the Billy Graham Evangelistic Association in 1972 and was used with great evangelistic success.

In 1972 Graham and Bill Bright of Campus Crusade for Christ put on their evangelistic Jesus Revolution extravaganza, Explo '72, in Dallas, Texas. With 150,000 in attendance, Graham addressed what he called "a religious Woodstock" with Cash and Cash's friend Kris Kristofferson as key performers. Cash sang "I've Seen Men Like Trees Walking," "A Thing Called Love," and "Supper Time." Graham and Cash also continued to grow closer, though Cash was still sporadically living out a painful legacy of depravity and despair. The golden-haired evangelist and the man in black seemed such an unlikely pair of friends.

CONSTANT COMPANION

Graham and Cash had a superficial connection based on their roots in the hardscrabble rural South. They grew up around Baptist churches and barns. Barbecue, cornbread, and pork and beans would set their mouths watering.

On a deeper level, though, their backgrounds couldn't have been more different. "Johnny came from the wild side, while Billy had never been through that phase. Billy walked the straight and narrow," observes Turner.

Even after his return to faith in 1967, Cash's life was pretty bumpy with what he called his "goof-ups." And when he slipped back into amphetamine usage, he could get out of control. Cash also felt let down by some of the ministries that he had latched on to for help. Turner says Cash felt that "some failed him, some exploited him."

So it was Graham's faithfulness and integrity that Cash gravitated toward. Graham was constant through the years, both in his personal relationship with Cash and in his theology. Graham didn't seem to go off on theological tangents at the drop of a dime. "Billy was a beacon to Cash who didn't change," says Turner. "Billy remained a stable character."

When Cash fell off the wagon, he likely didn't confide that to Graham, though June may well have shared it with Ruth. The two wives constantly prayed with each other over their husbands and children. Cash told Turner that in 1977 he was embarrassed that Graham would talk about the biography of the apostle Paul that Cash was writing, because he was too stoned to even write. In the 1980s there was a tabloid uproar over claims that Cash was having an affair and too stoned to appear at two Graham crusades. Cash denied the drug usage and said no one could separate him and June. However, Cash checked into a drug rehabilitation program.

Whether or not Graham knew all the details of Cash's "goof-ups," his response to Cash was as a loving friend, loyal through thick and thin. "Daddy stayed his friend, that's all," Franklin says. Cash's faith didn't change, but his closeness to God did. "Johnny never had problems with his faith, but he had problems with his life," Franklin observes. Billy continued to invite Cash to his crusades and, after Cash got clean from drugs, encouraged him to finally finish his book on Paul, *Man in White*, in 1986.

When Cash and Graham were together, it was like two brothers picking cotton together—one pretty steady and the other occasionally cutting up. Franklin says it was this southern sensibility that drew their relationship together once a foundation in Christ was set. "Johnny never lost his love of country, and neither had my father. The food they liked, the tastes they had," says Franklin. Johnny liked to bring the Grahams to his fishing cabin at Port Richey on the Pithla-chascotee River and to his old-style Jamaican house on Montego Bay. In the spring of 1976 after Cash had reportedly brewed coffee so strong you could barely drink it, Graham and Cash headed out to fish. They picked up shrimp, mullet, and squid for bait at Des Little's Fish Camp and spent the day casting lines, Scriptures, and songs.

These trips were a little primitive for the women. Ruth was always a little relieved to get back to the hotel in Jamaica after time at Cash's ramshackle place with creepy crawlies and loose boards. But wherever they were, the Grahams and Cashes were like family.

In their later years the couples talked to each other every week, sometimes every day. Graham was something of a hypochondriac and would get on the phone to update Cash on all the ailments that he had or might have. Cash would meet ailment for ailment until they would laugh together and pray for each other. When Ruth fell deathly sick one time, June spent six hours praying over her bedside. Cash's phone calls to Graham were often peppered with questions about the

Bible, some so difficult that the evangelist just counseled Johnny to ask God when he got to heaven.

Graham wrote Johnny a note after their first Christmas together, in 1974, that summarizes the many aspects of their relationship: "When we left, Ruth and I had tears in our eyes. . . . We have come to love you all as few people we have ever known. The fun we had, the delicious food we ate, the stimulating conversation, lying in the moonlight at night, the prayer meetings, the music we heard, etc. There has been running over and over in my mind 'Matthew 24 is knocking at the door.' I have a feeling this could be a big hit." Their friendship in Christ certainly was.

32

THE EVANGELIST OF OUR TIME

By the editors of *Christianity Today*

History will remember Billy Graham as the world's greatest missionary-evangelist. No other person has preached the gospel face-to-face to so many—over two hundred million. No other person has led so many to make explicit spiritual decisions, usually to accept Jesus Christ as Lord and Savior—over two million. And no other person has traveled to so many countries to preach the gospel—more than sixty-five.

How could it ever have happened? How could a shy country boy from the foothills of North Carolina sway millions and stand before kings?

Some have suggested that, at root, Billy Graham was a supreme opportunist. At a crucial point in Los Angeles in his early ministry, media tycoon William Randolph Hearst ordered his chain of newspapers to "Puff Graham." The media took over and created Billy Graham, his evangelistic career, and its worldwide success—or so the story goes.

Billy Graham's own answer to this puzzle, however, was "the hand of God." The Spirit of God fell on this unpromising material and called him to be an evangelist. And who can deny the evangelist was right? From the very first, Graham's unswerving purpose was to carry the message of the gospel to all the world—to everyone everywhere by whatever means—so that some might be saved from the guilt and burden of their sins and others aroused and strengthened to live obedient and useful lives for the glory of God. From that goal, he never deviated.

In his early mission, no doubt the heavy hand of William Randolph Hearst was laid upon him and gave him welcome advertising in his attempts to reach a wider public hearing. But even a superficial reading of Graham's ministry before that Los Angeles crusade (1949) will show a rising young evangelist of exceptional promise. Without Hearst, nationwide and worldwide acceptance might have proved slower in coming, but God's special call upon Billy Graham became clearly evident from the earliest days of his public ministry.

CRITICS ANSWERED

Graham never lacked critics both of his message and of his method. They came from right and left. Some charged him with the worst kind of opportunism: he warped the biblical gospel to whatever people wished to hear. It was alleged he taught an "easy believism": make a decision for Christ and you will be saved. Others reversed the charge and accused him of legalism: come forward, turn over a new leaf, and live a life separated from the world.

More serious was a charge by liberals and some evangelicals that he neglected the social implications of the gospel. The fact is, from his earliest days he stressed holy living and the duty of the regenerate believer to serve humankind. The piece of truth in this charge was that Graham laid less stress on political action—to build a better society by passing laws—than he did on right social conduct. The responsibility of the Christian to change society by legal action was always there, but he insisted that we shall never introduce a perfect society by passing laws (however necessary they are). The most important thing is to change people so they will want to structure society rightly and live for the good of others.

Particularly in the early days of his crusades, many fundamentalists and some evangelicals objected to the participation of liberal churches in his campaigns. Moreover, he did not challenge the distinctives of Roman Catholics; this his critics interpreted as ignoring the Reformation.

It is true, Graham rarely confronted liberals with their liberalism or attacked Roman Catholic distinctives. It was not that these teachings were unimportant to him, but they were clearly secondary. His call was to preach the gospel and the free grace of Christ, receivable on the condition of faith and faith alone. Graham believed that the good fruit borne by this preaching was ample confirmation that his method of presenting the truth positively was right. Countless disillusioned and spiritually starved liberals found life in the Savior through his crusades. And Roman Catholics usually made up the largest single denominational group attending his later citywide crusades.

As to his methodology, most criticism focused on the mass psychological appeal of his meetings, with their exuberant singing, intense testimonies by past converts, emotional appeal of the message, and the urgent pressure to come forward and "decide for Christ." Yet what strikes most people who actually attended his crusades and listened to his "invitations" was his lack of emotional tactics. Particularly in later years, his voice was calm, the words were simple, and the appeal reasonable. Most who objected to what was done really believed there is no legitimate role for an appeal to the will based on emotions, and thus forgot the wholeness of the human person.

Objections to the financial management of the crusades and the financial integrity of the crusade committee, especially of the Graham team, were almost nonexistent. The Graham organization kept meticulously accurate and detailed accounts that could be checked by all who made any contribution. Citywide committees were required to publish carefully audited accounts in local newspapers. And no one ever seriously questioned the financial integrity of Graham or those who worked with him.

A serious question raised by some, including a number of evangelicals, was the wisdom of citywide campaigns and the use of TV and radio to communicate the gospel. Were not these modern media-dominated events so expensive and, at the same time, so impersonal that they represented a misuse of kingdom resources?

In an increasingly secular society, however, some could be reached through mass evangelism who would never have darkened the door of a church. Who can measure how much the crusade "Schools for Evangelism" have built up the body of Christ? Or what spiritual blessings have come on the *Hour of Decision* through radio and television? The Christian works on the principle that everywhere and always, by all possible means, we seek to win the lost and strengthen the church.

A SUCCESSOR?

For Billy Graham, to live was to preach Christ. Now that he has been taken home to glory, where will mass evangelism go from here? With no crystal ball in which to gaze, we cannot answer that question.

Who will be his successor? No one! Jonathan Edwards had no successor. Neither did Whitefield or Wesley or Finney or Spurgeon or Moody or Billy Sunday or Walter Maier or Charles E. Fuller.

Billy Graham was an evangelist. In some ways he was "the evangelist." Certainly he was the evangelist of our time. God raised him up. And now that he has gone, it will be up to God to raise up another evangelist for another day.

Afterword

SEVEN THINGS I LEARNED FROM BILLY GRAHAM

By Rick Warren

B illy Graham is gone. This mighty man of God is now wrapped in the arms of his beloved redeemer. Yet this evangelist, counselor to world leaders, and unshakable beacon of integrity and stability has left deep footprints that will remain vivid to the entire world for generations to come. Those footprints have guided me throughout my ministry, and I follow them still. The influence of Billy Graham on my life is incalculable. I have the privilege of sharing with readers specific ways in which this great man influenced me personally. He impressed upon me seven vital lessons that have had much to do with the shaping of both my life and my ministry. And I believe these lessons will do much to reveal the key to what made Billy Graham what he has become to the world.

LESSON 1: MAINTAIN A LIFESTYLE OF INTEGRITY AND HUMILITY

The first thing Billy Graham taught me was to *maintain a lifestyle that God can bless*. He never let his character get soiled by a lot of things that have caused so many other pastors, ministers, and evangelists to fall. There are three common problems that usually cause leaders to fall. They are the three temptations of Jesus, the three temptations found in Genesis, and the three temptations of Moses in Hebrews 11. But they're best described in 1 John 2:16, where they are identified as the lust of the flesh, the lust of the eyes, and the pride of life. The lust of the flesh is the temptation to feel good. And by the way, that phrase means more than just sex. It could be any temptation that leads a person to say, "I deserve this; I ought to feel good." The lust of the eyes is the temptation "to have": that's greed.

And then there's that third temptation, the pride of life, which is the temptation to be recognized as important, accomplished, or superior. When people ask me, "What can I pray for you?" I always say, "Pray these three things—integrity, generosity, and humility, because those are the antidotes for those three great temptations." I watched Billy Graham deal gracefully with those three temptations his entire life.

When I was a little boy my grandmother lived with our family. She was a monthly supporter of Billy Graham, so she got his *Decision* magazine every month. Even at that age I would read that magazine and listen to Billy Graham's radio program, *Hour of Decision*.

I remember my grandmother telling me, "I pray for two people every day. I pray for Billy Graham, and I pray for you." She prayed for me because she always wanted me to be a pastor or a minister. Today I have no doubt that her prayers and the fact that Billy Graham was in our home every month with the magazine and every week on the radio did much to influence the direction my life took.

As I grew older, I began to understand Billy Graham's commitment to keeping his character clean—a commitment that a lot of people didn't seem to get. As a young pastor I understood why he and his staff made the Modesto Covenant to ensure the integrity of his ministry. Later, when I started Saddleback Church, our staff made similar covenants. We actually have a thing called the Saddleback Staff Ten Commandments, which are based on the idea Billy Graham had in making the Modesto Covenant with his team. As far as I was concerned, there wasn't any option. I said to my staff, "Look. We're going to do this." And we did. For example, we pledged never to be alone with a woman who was not our wife in a room with the door closed. And in twenty-seven years at Saddleback, I have never violated that commitment. A lot of people say, "You're being a little legalistic, aren't you?" And I always reply, "I'd rather go overboard than be thrown overboard."

Billy Graham lived that commitment to integrity and humility.

He maintained a humble lifestyle before God in spite of his enormous fame and success. He kept a simple home up there on the mountain. He took a salary instead of profits. He avoided all the excesses that we hate about the many evangelists who preach a prosperity gospel. A commitment to integrity is a crucial lesson for ministers to learn. And the reason I say it's important is that God doesn't bless a method; he blesses a man. He doesn't bless a strategy; he blesses a person. As E. M. Bounds said, "Men are God's method."

That's the first thing Billy Graham taught me: Watch your character, because given the right situation you could fall for anything. "Let him who thinks he stands take heed lest he fall" (1 Corinthians 10:12 NKJV). The moment you think you're beyond the temptation, you're going to be open for it. So I adopted a lot of things that he did to keep at arm's length the common temptations that ministers face.

LESSON 2: REACH BEYOND OUR EVANGELICAL BOUNDARIES

The second thing Billy Graham taught me is *the strategy of reaching out to those outside of evangelical bounds.* And he was a pro at this. In order to get the gospel to as many people as possible, he would build friendships, bridges, and alliances with people that those inside the evangelical boundaries often disapproved of. But he didn't care. He would put Catholics on his stage. He'd put political leaders on the stage, knowing that he would receive criticism for it.

Everything he did came out of his single focus. If ever there was a purpose-driven evangelist, it was Billy Graham. He never ever lost his focus. It was always the same: Bring people to Christ. Bring people to Christ. Bring people to Christ. And that is the number-one thing in my vocabulary, too. I'm not in it for politics; I'm not in it for fame; I'm not in it for climbing any ladder. The goal in everything we do at Saddleback is to make it easier for us to bring people to Jesus. That goal is what leads us to reach out and build bridges to Muslims, to Jews, and to the gay community. You reach out and build bridges to people who don't even like you. You build bridges of friendship from your heart to theirs so Jesus Christ can cross that bridge into their life.

Not long ago I spoke at the Biannual Conference of Reformed Judaism. To Orthodox Jews, Reformed Judaism is like the Episcopalians are to evangelicals. They're "lefty." I think I'm the first Protestant pastor ever invited to speak to that convention. It raised eyebrows among evangelicals. They wondered if I had gone off the deep end. But I didn't really care what the critics said because Paul says, "To the Jews I became like a Jew, to win the Jews. To those under the law I became like one under the law (though I myself am not under the law), so as to win those under the law. . . . To the weak I became weak, to win the weak. I have become all things to all people so that by all possible means I might save some" (1 Corinthians 9:20–22 NIV).

Billy Graham lived that principle to a *T.* We used that principle to build Saddleback, and we're now using it to reach out to major blocks of people around the world—like the one billion Muslims. So reaching out to those outside of evangelical bounds is a key lesson Billy Graham taught me.

LESSON 3: BROADEN THE AGENDA

The third thing I learned from Billy Graham is to *broaden the agenda*. Even though he was an evangelist at heart, he realized that the whole gospel must be taught. In so many ways he was a pioneer. Long before churches were ready for racial integration, he integrated his crusades. That's broadening the agenda.

The great evil of that generation was segregation. And he took it on. In broadening the agenda he did things like the Lausanne movement. He founded *Christianity Today* magazine; we needed an academic, respectable alternative to the *Christian Century*.

He was primarily an evangelist, but he used his enormous influence to say the church has to care about issues other than evangelism. The BGEA once produced a document that is basically the social conscience of Billy Graham. It is full of examples of things he did during the Cold War, during segregation, and during the rise of other issues that he felt strongly the church should address.

I admired Billy Graham's insistence on broadening the agenda so much that it affected my approach at Saddleback. We have broadened the agenda to take on the five global giants of poverty, disease, illiteracy, corruption in leadership, and spiritual emptiness. Like Billy Graham, we believe strongly in the primacy of evangelism. But also like him, we're just foolish enough to take on issues that show Christian love to a hurting and confused world.

LESSON 4: HAVE A GLOBAL VISION

The fourth thing Billy Graham taught me is to *have a global vision*. He was not just an evangelist to America. He cared about the whole world.

I remember when "Amsterdam '86"—the second Congress of Itinerant Evangelists—was coming up. I had written a book when I was in college called *Twelve Methods of Bible Study*, and it had been published in about sixteen or seventeen languages. You can imagine how floored I was when Billy called me one day and said, "I want you to come teach this to ten thousand evangelists." I agreed to do it, of course. And he bought ten thousand copies of my book and gave them free to every evangelist at that conference. It was a heady experience for a kid in his twenties to be invited by Billy Graham to teach evangelists from over the world how to study the Bible. Of course these were not prominent crusade evangelists. Many of them were itinerant preachers, church planters, or foot evangelists who walked from village to village.

The truly impressive lesson I learned from this experience was that a man with the power, visibility, and influence of Billy Graham could have had a comfortable career preaching Christ in his own nation. But his attention to the need for good Bible teaching around the globe made it obvious that he had a much larger vision. He was not willing to contain the gospel in his own back yard; he used his influence to spread the good news all over the globe. He did this in his crusades, in conferences, in meetings with leaders, and with opportunities such as Amsterdam '86.

LESSON 5: MAINTAIN A SINGLE FOCUS

The fifth lesson I learned from Billy Graham is to *never lose your single focus*. His focus was always on bringing people to Christ. I remember when Billy received the Congressional Gold Medal in the rotunda of the U.S. Capitol. There were about four hundred chairs, jam-packed with VIPs who had been invited from all over America and around the world. President Clinton and leaders of the House and Senate addressed the crowd, honoring Billy Graham's life and achievements. And what do you think Billy did when it came time for him to get up to speak? Instead of talking about his long ministry and memories and the honor he was receiving, he spent maybe three minutes acknowledging the honor and how little he deserved it. And then he said, "Let me tell you about Jesus." In the rest of his speech he gave the same simple presentation of the plan of salvation that we've all heard him give over and over and over. He was not going to miss an opportunity. Even though the entire event was about him, he turned the meeting toward his lifetime central focus: Jesus.

And God honored that single focus. I remember sitting there in the Capitol rotunda with tears coming down my cheeks as I thought,

Thank you, God, for a guy who never misses a beat, never loses a chance to share the good news.

LESSON 6: USE THE LATEST TECHNOLOGY

Another thing Billy Graham taught me is to *take advantage of the latest technology.* He never gave up looking for new ways to share the gospel. And not only did he use the latest technology, he used multiple technologies to get the message across. Let me give you an early example.

In the Harringay Crusade back in 1954, he used telephones. The building leased for the crusade wouldn't hold everybody, so they piped his sermons into phone lines using a telephone relay system that had been invented for use in World War II. People all over England took their phones off the hook and sat in small groups listening to his message.

And that was just the beginning. He was always asking what technology or media could be used to get the word out. So he started *Decision* magazine. He started World Wide Pictures, doing Christian movies when fundamentalists were still fighting movies. He started *Christianity Today* magazine. He wrote books. He wrote articles. He did radio and audiotapes. He did simulcasts. In fact, he did the first global simulcast from Puerto Rico, reaching a billion people in Latin American countries. He never stopped looking for new ways to preach the gospel. Today you can even download an iPhone app and an Android app from the BGEA website. Someone quoted Billy Graham as saying, "It's not about how many people I can get into the stadium, but how many people I can get the word out to." And that was something very important I learned from him.

At Saddleback we have tried to follow Mr. Graham's philosophy. In about 1982 Saddleback was the first church to use a fax machine for evangelism. I came up with a thing called "the fax of life." I wrote a weekly devotional, and we faxed it out to business leaders. And then they would fax it on.

Billy learned of what we were doing and wrote me a note saying, "This is really good. Using the fax machine to get the word out is a great idea." Saddleback was the first church on the Internet. That was in 1992, before Internet Explorer, Netscape, or Safari. We used technologies called Gopher and FDP and Mosaic out of the University of Cincinnati, and we put up a little website. Some time ago I bought everybody on staff an iPod, and we started using iPods for early stages of training. Following Billy Graham's example, we're always just looking for technical ways to get the gospel out. We're now looking at text messaging, because while not everybody is going to have a laptop or an Internet connection, over two billion people now have cell phones. And that number is growing rapidly.

I was in Jakarta just a few years ago, and I asked a Christian leader there, "How many text messages do you get a day?" He said, "Oh, hundreds, because that's the way we communicate. We don't call each other. We text each other. I took notes on your sermon as you preached and text messaged it to all of my friends. Oh, and here's our daily devotional that just came through." The man had actually Black-Berryied my sermon while I was preaching it, sending it out to multiple people who would not have heard it otherwise. That is just one example of how we can use developing technology.

LESSON 7: BUILD YOUR MINISTRY ON A TEAM

The seventh thing I learned from Billy Graham is to *build your ministry on a team.* Team ministry. No one can ever do it by himself. Billy Graham knew this, and he built a core team that was with him for fifty years. Everybody on the team brought strengths to the table. When you build an effective team, you hire people who compensate for your weaknesses and who mobilize or reinforce your strengths, because nobody can be good at everything. When you have a team that stays together fifty years, you have no ego anymore. You can read each other's minds. I have sat onstage behind Cliff Barrows when Billy was up preaching, and it was clear that Cliff knew exactly what Billy was going to do. And Billy knew exactly what his staff would do, because they had been together for so long.

That's the way I am with my worship leaders. I've got guys who have been with me now for twenty-five years. Rick Muchow can read my mind. When I am preaching he knows exactly where I'm going, and he's going to have the music right there at the right time. When you work together long enough, you know each other's minds. So I think that whole idea of team ministry has been a good model for us. In fact, we've frequently referred to the Billy Graham team as a model for our core guys.

THE INFLUENCE OF BILLY GRAHAM THE MAN

These seven lessons I learned from Billy Graham have been invaluable to me. But even above these clearly identifiable monoliths of wisdom, I am convinced that the greatest influence the man had on me came not from what he taught but simply from who he was.

In his later years he gave me excellent and expert counsel I believe I could have gotten from no one else. I would often call him and ask, "What do I do about this?" I knew of no one else I could talk to who had dealt with some of the things I was facing. When my book *The Purpose Driven Life* came out, I began getting invitations from church leaders, business leaders, government leaders, and other influencers who wanted me to talk to their groups. I did not know how to handle myself in all these arenas, so I'd get my list of questions and I'd call up Billy Graham. "Okay," I would ask, "what do I say to this group? What do I do in that situation? How do you handle the criticism on this point?" And he gave me excellent advice because he was a pro at knowing just how to communicate effectively in so many arenas.

Whenever anybody says, "Who's going to replace Graham?" the answer is that he's irreplaceable. There will never be another Billy Graham. Just as there will never be another Martin Luther. Billy Graham was Billy Graham. Whether crusade evangelism can have the same effect now as it did in years past, I don't know. But I do know that God raised him up.

Acts 13:36, which is my life verse, is an appropriate passage to describe Billy Graham. It says, "Now when David had served God's purpose in his own generation, he fell asleep" (NIV). I can't think of a finer epitaph to have on your tombstone than that you served God's purpose in your generation. That says you did the timeless in a timely way. You contended for that which never changes, in a society, in a world, in a culture that's constantly changing. Billy Graham served God's purpose in his generation, and now that he has fulfilled that purpose, he is gone.

Billy Graham cannot be replaced. I can see him in his son Franklin Graham. I can see him in his daughter Anne Graham Lotz; but no one is going to step into his shoes and be Billy Graham any more than anyone else could be John Calvin. Some people are historically unique. God raised them up to serve his purpose in their time.

While I have many fine memories of Billy Graham, I think the greatest may have been something that struck me at the New York Crusade, which was his last. I was watching him observe the people after he had given the invitation. Most pastors do not have the courage to call for commitment and then just wait it out while people decide to respond. Every sermon really comes down to two words: *will you?* The only thing that differs in each sermon is what you're asking them to do. Will you give your life to Christ? Will you surrender in full obedience? Will you go to the mission field? Will you become a disciple?

Will you be a good father? Regardless of the subject, it comes down to the invitation.

Part of the brilliance of Billy Graham was that he understood how to draw the net. A lot of great preachers don't. They preach really good sermons but they don't know how to call for commitment. It takes courage to stand up there and say, "Will you do this?" and then just wait.

I had watched Billy Graham do this for years. But in that last crusade it was really special to see him sitting there in that custom-made pulpit equipped with a chair because he could no longer stand through an entire message. He looked every bit like a magnificent eagle. It was almost as if he was perched on this chair looking out with his long, white mane of hair and the sharp nose and jutting jaw that made him so handsome for so many years. Again and again he would look from one side, to the middle, and to the other side without saying a word. To me he seemed like a grand eagle just looking out there and saying to himself, *God, you are working.*

On one of the nights in that New York crusade, he had given the invitation and there were hundreds of respondents standing at the front, waiting quietly. Suddenly one man broke out into praying aloud, quite loud. We really couldn't hear what he was saying, but he was crying out to God with real emotion. It was distracting enough that you might expect security to be summoned to quiet the guy down or escort him off the field. But Billy didn't squelch the outburst. He didn't try to redirect it. He didn't have security come and get the guy. I'll never forget what he said: "Now, let that guy be. I've learned that sometimes God is moving in an amazing way, and we don't know what's going on. So just let him be." There was an enormous treasure in those words that came from the wisdom of experience. Billy Graham knew that sometimes God will do something that cannot be explained, and he was willing to just stand there and let that happen.

Years ago I went to San Diego to help in a Billy Graham crusade at Jack Murphy Stadium. He preached a message on loneliness entitled, "I Am a Pelican in the Wilderness." To be honest, it was really just an average message, maybe even on the verge of being disjointed. But when he got to the invitation, *boom!* The power of God fell. I firmly believe this was God blessing the life of a man. The power of God in Billy Graham's life was such that he could have gotten up and preached "Mary Had a Little Lamb" and people would have come forward. He was the embodiment of the Latin proverb, "Whose life is as lightning, his words are as thunder." This man's integrity and lifestyle were so right and his heart was so directed by God that it came through in his words and presence. That direction of a man's heart is more important than having a great sermon. Indeed, it *is* a great sermon. The sermon Billy Graham preached was his life.

People talk about Billy Graham the preacher. But I think Billy Graham the leader and Billy Graham the model will even outlast the sermons. Who he was will turn out to be even more important than what he said.

Notes

CHAPTER 10: THE REVOLUTIONARY GOSPEL

1. D. T. Niles, *That They May Have Life* (New York: Harper and Brothers, 1951).

CHAPTER 11: THE CRUCIAL IMPORTANCE OF EVANGELISM

1. Population Reference Bureau's 2010 World Population Data Sheet.

2. James S. Stewart, *Heralds of God* (New York: Charles Scribner's Sons, 1946).

3. David Brainerd, *The Life and Diary of David Brainerd with Notes and Reflections*, ed. Jonathan Edwards.

4. George Smith, *Henry Martyn: Saint and Scholar* (London: The Religious Tract Society, 1892), 224.

CHAPTER 13: MAXIMIZING THE MESSAGE AND THE METHOD

1. W. E. Sangster, *Let Me Commend: Realistic Evangelism* (New York: Abingdon-Cokesbury Press, 1948).

CHAPTER 19: CHOOSE LEADERS WHO RELY ON GOD

1. Marquis James, *The Raven: The Life Story of Sam Houston* (New York: Blue Ribbon Books, 1929).

CHAPTER 20: RECOVER THE PRIORITY OF EVANGELISM

1. Michael Green, *Evangelism Through the Local Church* (Nashville, TN: Thomas Nelson, Inc., 1992).

2. George Hunter, quoted in Bill Hull, *Can We Save the Evangelical Church? The Lion Has Roared* (Grand Rapids, MI: Fleming H. Revell, 1993).

CHAPTER 21: RESPOND TO THE HARVEST

1. Niels Jørgen Cappelørn and Jon Stewart, eds., *Kierkegaard Revisited: Proceedings from the Conference "Kierkegaard and the Meaning of Meaning It"* (Berlin: Walter de Gruyter & Co., 1997), 105.

About the Author

B illy Graham, born in 1918 in Charlotte, North Carolina, preached to more people in live audiences than anyone else in history—nearly 215 million people in more than 185 countries and territories—from New York's Central Park to the African bush. Hundreds of millions more were reached through his television, video, film, and webcasts.

He helped launch numerous organizations such as Youth for Christ, the Billy Graham Evangelistic Association, and *Christianity Today,* and played a significant role in the development of the Evangelical Council for Financial Accountability, Greater Europe Mission, Trans World Radio, World Vision, World Relief, and the National Association of Evangelicals. He also wrote more than thirty books that were translated into dozens of languages, including several *New York Times* and Christian Booksellers Association bestsellers.

Ever considered a model of integrity, Graham was named by the Gallup organization as one of the "Ten Most Admired Men in the World" more than fifty times during his lifetime—a number that is unparalleled. He also appeared on the covers of *Time, Newsweek, Life,* and a host of other magazines in addition to being the subject of many newspaper features and articles.

Together Billy and his wife, Ruth, had three daughters, two sons, nineteen grandchildren, and numerous great-grandchildren. They were married for more than sixty years until her death in 2007.